LAYMAN'S GUIDE TO

AMOS

THE COUNTRY PREACHER

BRAD THOMPSON

1611 Publications llc

Brad Thompson

All Scripture taken from the King James Bible

1611publications@gmail.com

1611 Publications
P.O. Box 105
Florien, La. 71429

ISBN: 978-1-970984-00-2

Cover Design by Brad Thompson
Edited by Jennifer Thompson

Table of Contents

Dedication

I have always had the desire to write, but never thought that I had the ability to do so. For years my dad had planned to write a book on the history of Israel. He compiled information, and kept tremendous notes, but never got around to writing the book. In 2020 he was diagnosed with Parkinson's disease. His condition has left him unable to finish the work that he started. In the middle of 2025 he and I agreed that I would take his work, build on it, and write his book on Israel. Although I have found it to be more difficult than I anticipated to take his work and finish it, working on his book has opened my eyes to my love for writing. So this first book is dedicated to my dad, John Thompson jr. A man that I have watched studied the bible tirelessly for years.

Acknowledgements

I could not let this book go to print without saying thank you to my wife of almost 25 years. She works from sun up till sun down taking care of me and our 4 sons. She's gotten 3 of them through 12 years of homeschooling. While still having 1 left in school, she has still found time to help me proof read and edit the manuscripts for this book. I truly could not have done this without you Jennifer! I love you sweetheart!

Introduction

Amos was the first character that I studied when I started reading the minor prophets. The similarities between Israel in Amos' day and America in our day has always amazed me! There truly is nothing new under the sun!

As you come to the time of Amos, Israel and Judah have been divided for almost 200 years. Israel has grown into two distinct groups, the very wealthy and the very poor. We read in the book of II Kings chapter 14 when Jeroboam II began to reign in Israel, he conquered land previously lost to Israel increasing their borders, and bringing financial success to the upper class. Because of this prosperity, and the pagan worship that they were founded upon under Jeroboam I in the book of I Kings chapter 12, they were perfectly happy with a *"form of godliness"* while pursuing their materialistic goals (sound familiar)?

God calls this man by the name of Amos, a man with no formal education, no money, no background in the priesthood, and no couth or tact! However, Amos did possess something that Israel did not have, and that was a burning desire to please his Heavenly Father!

Amos arrives in Israel and begins fearlessly preaching God's message of Judgment to the comfortable, worldly Hebrews that were living in Israel.

Chapter 1 we have a brief introduction to Amos before being dropped right in the middle of his preaching to Israel. Amos begins by proclaiming God's judgment against Israel's enemies. Amos addresses Damascus, Gaza, Tyrus, Edom, and Ammon all in chapter 1. Each address starts the same way, *"for three transgressions or for four."* Each address is only 2 to 3 verses long, and each address ends the same way, judgment.

Chapter 2 Amos continues to deliver God's message of Judgment to their wicked family. Moab were distant cousins to Israel. Chapter 2 starts with God's proclamation against them. Amos then turns his attention to the 2 southern tribes of Judah in verses 4 and 5 before ultimately turning to the main reason that God has sent him there, Israel. Amos focuses his preaching on Israel in Amos 2:6, and his attention will stay there for the remainder of the book.

Chapter 3 Amos asks Israel a series of rhetorical questions that are meant to get their attention and make them think. The point of these questions is this, how can they expect God not to bring judgment in their lives? They have mocked God's laws forsake his commandments all while making light of the commands of God!

Chapter 4 Amos starts by addressing the women in the city, the ones who were really calling the shots behind the scene as they whispered their commands in the ears of their panty wearing husbands. (Yes, you read that right). God deliver us from this generation of soft men! We need a generation of men who will rise up and lead their families in the ways of God! The remainder of the chapter is Amos cataloging everything that God has done to get their attention. Amos lists 5 things that God had brought into the lives of Israel to get their attention. Sadly, we see that none of these things worked because Amos ends each of these different events with the following statement, *"yet have ye not returned unto me, saith the LORD."*

Chapter 5 starts out with a lamentation. Amos is mourning the fact that this generation that he is preaching to will fall and will *"no more rise."* In this chapter Amos admonishes Israel not to seek after Bethel, Gilgal, or Beer-sheba, but to seek after God. All three of these places were once places that were known for the power and presence of God, but they have ultimately been corrupted by man. So Amos' message is this, don't seek after what looks like God but seek after God himself!

Chapter 6 Amos starts with a Woe! He's giving a warning to those that have grown at ease and are comfortable with sin. This is a chapter that reminds us that there is pleasure in sin, but it is only for a fleeting season. Soon, that season of pleasure will be over and the time to pay will arrive.

Chapter 7 Amos tells of two events that happen, the swarm of grasshoppers (locust) and a fire. Both times God was ready to pour his judgment out and both times Amos intercedes on behalf of Israel. This dialog is interrupted by a personal attack against Amos by the priest named Amaziah. This is not a godly priest, but a priest that was one picked from the *"lowest of the people,"* I Kings 12:31. Amaziah lies about Amos, and tells him to go back where he came from. As you read the end of the chapter you'll find that Amaziah paid a high price for his words against the prophet of God.

Chapter 8 Amos gets back to his judgments that he began in the previous chapter. Both in chapter 7 and again in chapter 8 God asks Amos the question, *"What seest thou."* Basically what God is telling Amos here is this, there have been two times that Amos has interceded on behalf of Israel, and God did not bring judgment on Israel based completely on the prayer of Amos. But now God will no longer give mercy based solely on the prayer of Amos. If Israel wants mercy from God they will have to repent.

We also see in this chapter their insincerity and their form of religion. They are keeping their feasts and sacrifices, unfortunately these feasts and sacrifices are not based on the commands of God but based on the false worship that Jeroboam I set up in I Kings 12. Even in these false feasts, we see their half hearted worship. *"Saying when will the new moon be gone, that we may sell corn? And the sabbath, that we may set forth wheat, making the ephah small, and the shekel great, and falsifying the balances by deceit?"* Amos 8:5

In chapter 9 we see that they will not escape the wrath of God. The first part of this chapter brings to mind what God told them hundreds of years earlier.

Numbers 32:23

But if ye will not do so, behold, ye have sinned against the LORD: and be sure your sin will find you out.

But I'm glad that is not where the story ends, because we see at the end of this chapter that God is not done with Israel. He tells them that they will be sifted through the nations, but they will not be lost in this sifting, and that one day God will restore Israel again!

CHAPTER 1

The Call of God

Amos 1:1

The words of Amos, who was among the herdmen of Tekoa, which he saw concerning Israel in the days of Uzziah king of Judah, and in the days of Jeroboam the son of Joash king of Israel, two years before the earthquake.

That's it. No degree from the local synagogue, no ringing endorsement from the dean of the nationally acclaimed Bible college of their day. Just a man with a heart for God and a call on his life, and that's ALL you need!

I'm not saying that preparation is not important, I'm not saying that education is not important. The Bible is very clear that a novice should not be in the ministry. But I'm afraid we are adopting the philosophies of the world in that we give special clout to those who have an education from a popular Bible college, and tend to look down our nose at the young man who was raised in a good Bible believing church and trained at the feet of his pastor. But I digress.

Amos was a simple country preacher. No formal education, a herdman, and a gatherer of sycamore fruit as he so eloquently stated in Chapter 7.

Amos 7:14

Then answered Amos, and said to Amaziah, I was no prophet, neither was I a prophet's son; but I was an herdman, and a gatherer of sycomore fruit:

Allow me to set the scene for you. Amos lived in the land of Tekoa which was about 10-12 miles southeast of Jerusalem in the southern kingdom of Judah. The events of the book of Amos take place almost two hundred years after the split of the kingdom.

We do not know the age of Amos, but I would imagine him to be a middle age man. He is not a young man given to impulse. He is not an old man withered and crippled. But a man with enough life experience to know right from wrong, and enough youth to be able to do something about it.

We can gather from the writings of Amos, that he had a tremendous love and zeal for his God, and the laws of his God. It will be painfully evident as you read through the book of Amos that the majority of those that lived in Israel, and even in Judah, did not share Amos' enthusiasm.

Amos, being someone who took the commandments of God very seriously, would take three of these twelve mile trips to Jerusalem a year. This was the command given in Deuteronomy 16 to observe the feasts that God laid out for them in Leviticus chapter 23.

Deuteronomy 16:16

Three times in a year shall all thy males appear before the LORD thy God in the place which he shall choose; in the feast of unleavened bread, and in the feast of weeks, and in the feast of tabernacles: and they shall not appear before the LORD empty:

I can imagine these being very serious and somber times in Amos' life, as he understood the weight of the feasts, and what they represented. Amos would get to Jerusalem, and no doubt be grieved in his spirit as he would hear the conversations. Conversations that did not revolve around their great love for God, how good God has been in their lives, or how unworthy they were to be so blessed by the God of Heaven. Their conversations would revolve around their business, and their love of making money.

Amos 8:5

Saying, When will the new moon be gone, that we may sell corn? and the sabbath, that we may set forth

wheat, making the ephah small, and the shekel great, and falsifying the balances by deceit?

These men could not wait for the feast days to be over, so they could get back to their business of making money. Much like many baptists today who cannot wait for church to be over so they can get to their ball game, or have no problem with volunteering for overtime on Sundays so they can afford their newest toy or gadget. The sacred holy days of God had little impact on the conscience of most in Israel.

According to Leviticus, God commanded that when they were to bring sacrifices, they were not to bring the halt, the maimed, or the spotted from their flocks, but they were to bring the very best of their livestock for a sacrifice to God. However, I would imagine men with the attitude of those exhibited in the previously mentioned verse (Amos 8:5) wouldn't bat an eye at bringing God the leftovers. (I think there's an application to be made there)!!!

After the feast days are over, and Amos begins the 12 mile journey back home, the events of the feasts play in his mind. Israel's insincerity and their disregard for God's commands ate at Amos.

Amos would get home and quite possibly, even as soon as the next day, begin inspecting his sheep. Seeing which ones were the best. So he could set them aside for an offering to God the following year.

As a farmer, Amos would be well aware of God's command to let the land rest on the seventh year. And as a faithful servant of God, Amos was determined to do just that. I could imagine that Amos would look around on that seventh year, and see his neighbors disregarding the commands of God, and reaping bumper crops.

No doubt they would make fun of Amos. "*Come on, Amos! God isn't concerned if you plant on the seventh year or not, look how God is blessing us!*" Now obviously I was not there and do not know exactly how all these events played out, but the book of Amos makes it pretty clear that God used the zeal of Amos, and the coldness of Israel, to bring Amos to the point of surrendering to the call of God on his life.

Although Amos lived in Judah, the primary focus of Amos' ministry was to the ten northern tribes of Israel. It is also interesting that Israel has come full circle. Years ago, the kingdoms spilt. The southern tribes of Judah and Benjamin, known only as Judah, stayed with Rehoboam, Solomon's son. While the other ten tribes known as Israel, defected and went with Jeroboam.

Now, almost 200 years later, Israel has another king by the name of Jeroboam. But spiritually it has been a rough 200 years. The first Jeroboam quickly introduced idolatry into the kingdom (II Kings 12). There have been scandals, wicked kings (Ahab), and a complete disregard for the commands and laws of God. And God has had enough!

Hebrews 10:31

It is a fearful thing to fall into the hands of the living God.

You see, years before Paul wrote Hebrews 10:31God had an Amos warning of His wrath. Some would say he's just a farmer. Some would say he's just a herdsman on the backside of nowhere. But keep in mind, God always prepares his men in solitude!

Moses in the wilderness, Paul in the Arabian desert, David in the back forty watching his fathers sheep. God always preps his greatest servants in solitary confinement.

The Surrender

We do not know how long Amos wrestled with God's call on his life. Was it a long drawn out struggle, with Amos questioning God? Did he surrender quickly when God put the burden on his life? We do not know the answers to these questions, but we do know that after Amos surrendered, he was fully invested!

Amos left his home in Tekoa, and traveled the 10-12 miles up to Jerusalem. However, Amos did not stop there. He continued north until he had come into the territory of Israel.

In the days that we live in with convenient and quick transportation we think little of traveling far from home. But it is quite likely that Amos had never been this far away from home. Although he was still technically among family, I'm sure Amos still had a knot in the pit of his stomach as he realized where he was, who he was around, and the message that he was about to proclaim.

Amos was not the first prophet that God released on Israel, nor was he the only one prophesying at this time. It's quite possible that Amos, Hosea, and Isaiah all knew of each other, and knew each other well. Because they all lived during the same period of time.

There are some interesting details that we can compare and contrast between Amos and Hosea. Hosea's ministry approached Israel from the point of God's disappointment and heartache over Israel's spiritual adultery. While Amos' approach was quite different, Amos' message was, *"God's mad, and you're in a heap of trouble."*

The Message

We do not know what city Amos walks into first. Perhaps Bethel, perhaps Samaria. Regardless Amos walks into town, and begins to preach God's judgment. But he does it a little differently than most prophets did in that day. Usually prophets would begin by calling out the sins of Israel, and then call out the sins of their enemies. But Amos did not follow this pattern. Amos started by calling out the sins of the enemies of Israel.

Amos starts his street preaching ministry by stating that God is about to make His presence known!

Amos 1:2

And he said,The LORD will roar from Zion, and utter his voice from Jerusalem; and the habitations of the shepherds shall mourn, and the top of Carmel shall wither.

Amos is, in essence, saying that God has been silent for quite some time, and the terror of His wrath is imminent. When a lion is stalking his prey, he is quiet, he is stealthy. He creeps up in silence, giving his victim a false sense of security. The lion only roars when he knows that his victim is caught, and has no chance of escape. Our Lord's proclamation of judgment is not an empty threat. He has roared! He has spoken! It will come to pass!

Ezekiel 24:14

I the LORD have spoken it: it shall come to pass, and I will do it; I will not go back, neither will I spare, neither will I repent; according to thy ways, and according to thy doings, shall they judge thee, saith the Lord GOD.

In my mind, I can see Amos picking out a random street corner, and just start preaching the message the Lord has given him. A crowd begins to gather, because they like what Amos is saying. Much like our churches of today, we really get into the message if it is calling out the sins of others.

In the first and second chapter, Amos delivers short, two to three verse judgments to seven different nations before he gets to the main message he is sent there to deliver. I want you to notice the common thread that runs through all of them.

He starts out each judgment (Amos 1:3, 1:6, 1:9, 1:11, 1:13, 2:1, 2:4, 2:6) in the exact same way, *"Thus saith the Lord, for three transgressions….. or for four."* First of all notice that these are not Amos' messages, they are God's messages. *"Thus saith the Lord."* You may disagree with a man's delivery, or you may not like his personality, but when a man is preaching precepts and principles that are clearly spelled out in scripture, you'd better take heed!

Secondly, notice he tells each nation, *"for three transgressions, or for four."* Obviously each of these nations have transgressed God's law, not three times, not four times, not even seven times, but hundreds of times. I believe we are seeing a little bit of the sarcastic attitude of Amos, (this is not the only time his sarcasm is evident). I believe that this is Amos' way of telling them that God has had abundant mercy, and given many opportunities to get right. God is a merciful God. He is a gracious God. But there comes a time when that mercy and grace comes to an end. Amos is telling them that they are about to go over the edge of the cliff of God's wrath.

The Enemy from the North

Amos 1:3

Thus saith the LORD; For three transgressions of Damascus, and for four, I will not turn away the punishment thereof; because they have threshed Gilead with threshing instruments of iron:

4 But I will send a fire into the house of Hazael, which shall devour the palaces of Benhadad.

5 I will break also the bar of Damascus, and cut off the inhabitant from the plain of Aven, and him that holdeth the sceptre from the house of Eden: and the people of Syria shall go into captivity unto Kir, saith the LORD.

Damascus is the capital city of Syria. Although the conflicts between Syria and Israel were many, Amos points out one instance in particular.

Over one hundred years before Amos is giving his warning to Israel. Ahab was king in the land. In I Kings 19, Elijah is on the run from Jezebel after having won a great victory for God on Mt. Carmel. Towards the end of that chapter God gives Elijah three commands. Listing them in reverse order from I Kings 19, God tells Elijah to anoint Elisha as his replacement. To anoint Jehu as king of Israel. And probably the oddest command of the three, to anoint Hazael as king over Syria.

Elijah only fulfills one of the commands. And that is to anoint his successor, Elisha. He did this, not because he was in rebellion, but because the other two commands were put on hold by God when Ahab humbled himself after hearing God's judgment against him in I Kings 21.

In II Kings 2, we have Elijah going to heaven in a chariot of fire. Elisha, picking up his mantle, will later fulfill the last two commandments that were left unfulfilled by Elijah. In II Kings 5 there is the story of Naaman being healed of leprosy by God through Elisha. Naaman was the captain of the host of the king of, you guess it, Syria.

In II Kings 8, Elisha walks into Damascus, Benhadad, King of Syria, was sick. Obviously Benhadad knew of the leprosy of the captain of his army, Naaman. And no doubt Benhadad had heard about Elisha from Naaman after Naaman had been cleansed of his leprosy. So when Benhadad hears that Elisha is in Damascus, he is excited. Because he sees an opportunity to be healed just as Naaman was. So Benhadad sends word to Elisha by a man named Hazael.

Elisha tells Hazael that Benhadad would recover. But then begins to weep. When Hazael asks why Elisha is weeping, Elisha tells Hazael all the evils that he will commit against the nation of Israel (II Kings 8:12). Hazael acts shocked at this seemingly unsubstantiated accusation. But just a few verses later, after Elisha revealed that he would be King of Syria, Hazael kills Benhadad. He ascends to the throne of Syria, and then goes on to do exactly what Elisha foretold he would do. Amos recounts this over one hundred and twenty years later and sites this as being a major factor in Gods judgment against Syria. Israel may have forgotten what Syria did to them. Syria may have forgotten what they did to Israel, but God has a perfect memory.

The Enemy to the South

Amos 1:6-8

6 Thus saith the LORD; For three transgressions of Gaza, and for four, I will not turn away the punishment thereof; because they carried away captive the whole captivity, to deliver them up to Edom:

7 But I will send a fire on the wall of Gaza, which shall devour the palaces thereof:

8 And I will cut off the inhabitant from Ashdod, and him that holdeth the sceptre from Ashkelon, and I will turn mine hand against Ekron: and the remnant of the Philistines shall perish, saith the Lord GOD.

This is the most recognized enemy of Israel even though it's not evident at first glance, because just as Amos did with the previous judgment of Syria. He doesn't call them out by the name of their nation, but by one of their capital cities.

Gaza is a city of the Philistines. Along with the other three that are mentioned in these verses, Ashdod, Askelon, and Ekron. However, there is one city that is missing from this list. Gath has already been destroyed. II Chronicles 26 tells us that King Uzziah came to the throne of Judah and destroyed Gath. Uzziah reigned for 52 years, and is still on the throne of Judah when Amos prophesies. He will mention the ruin of Gath briefly in chapter 6.

Ashdod is the first city mentioned by Amos. It is mentioned 18 times in scripture. He says that the inhabitants shall be *"cut off."* No further information is given by Amos as to why. So anything that is said any further than this is purely speculation. But I suppose it could be because of idolatry and mishandling of the ark of the covenant.

In I Samuel 5 when Israel is at war with the Philistines, they are losing in battle. Instead of getting right with God, they bring out the Ark of the Covenant and parade it around like some lucky charm supposing that God is obligated to win the battle for them because they have the Ark. This is sadly the tactics of many Christian's today. They want to live in their wickedness, but claim the promises of God when they are in the proverbial pickle. If we do this we are soon to find out what Israel found out. That God doesn't work that way.

Read I Samuel 5 and you'll find that Israel was defeated, and the Ark was taken. Remember how it was placed in the house of Dagon? This was in the city of Ashdod!

Ashkelon is the next city mentioned as a target of God's judgment by Amos. It's interesting that Ashkelon does not show up at all in the books of Samuel, Kings, or Chronicles. It is only mentioned seven times by the prophets, Jeremiah, Amos, Zephaniah, and Zachariah. Only one historical book holds a direct reference to Ashkelon, and it appears only once. That is the book of the Judges chapter 14. It was the story of Sampson where he slew thirty men after they got the answer to his riddle from his wife.

Ekron is the third and final Philistine city that Amos mentions. Ekron is mentioned twenty times in scripture. It is the city that the Philistines send the Ark of the Covenant to after it left Ashdod. In II Kings chapter 1, Ahaziah fell through the lattice in his chamber. He sent to enquire, not of God, but of Baalzebub, and he calls him the god of Ekron.

Obviously, there is a very colorful and turbulent past between Israel and the Philistines. Even though God's anger is hot against Israel, and they are going to be judged for their sins, that did not cancel out God's judgment against the Philistines. They were still going to answer for their sins!

We started out by envisioning Amos preaching on a street corner in Samaria. I can see Amos as he begins pronouncing God's judgment against Syria, a crowd begins to form. They like to hear preaching on other peoples sins. (I guess some things never change). A few heads nod in agreement, and a few amens come from the back of the crowd.

Amos moves on to God's judgment of the Philistines, and the amens get louder, the crowd gets more enthusiastic as more and more judgment is pronounced against Israel's enemies.

The Enemy That Abandons

Amos 1:9-10

9 Thus saith the LORD; For three transgressions of Tyrus, and for four, I will not turn away the punishment thereof; because they delivered up the whole captivity to Edom, and remembered not the brotherly covenant:

10 But I will send a fire on the wall of Tyrus, which shall devour the palaces thereof.

The first two nations, Syria and Philistia, are obvious, long standing thorns in the flesh of Israel. But with Tyrus, Amos' judgments takes a different twist. Amos makes an interesting observation. *"They remembered not the brotherly covenant"* (vs 9).

An attack by a known enemy is expected. It may hurt, but it is more easily dealt with. But an attack from a friend? Those wounds go deep. This is the case with Tyrus. They were once friends with Israel.

In II Samuel 5, David is ascending to the throne of Israel. In verse 11 of that chapter, the Bible tells us that Hiram, king of Tyre sent lumber, and carpenters, and masons, and built David a house.

Years later, after David had died, Solomon came to the throne of Israel. The Bible says that Hiram sent two servants to Solomon not because he was afraid of Solomon and was trying to get in good with the new king of Israel. But verse 1of I Kings 5 specifically says that Hiram loved David.

There was a bond. There was a friendship there that ran deep between David and Hiram. That friendship extended to Solomon after the death of David. But somewhere along the line that friendship was forgotten. Israel was backstabbed in battle, and they were delivered captive to the Edomites by the hand of Tyrus.

The most painful wounds, and the deepest hurt, comes not from the known enemy, but from the assumed friend.

Psalms 55:12

For it was not an enemy that reproached me; then I could have borne it:

neither was it he that hated me that did magnify himself against me; then I would have hid myself from him:

Amos is preaching God's judgment against Damascus, against Syria. The Crowd grows, and the amens get louder. But when Amos begins pronouncing God's judgment against Tyre, I can imagine that the crowd is stirred to a fever pitch.

But now, the focus changes, and hits even closer to home. In Amos' judgment against Damascus and Gaza, it was expected, even praised. In his judgment against Tyrus, it was celebrated as revenge against a backstabbing best friend. But the next three announcements of God's judgment were even juicier for Israel.

These next three were against *"that other side of the family."* These were distant relatives of Israel, that they never did get along with. (And you thought your family was dysfunctional).

The Enemy that is Related

Amos 1:11-12

11 Thus saith the LORD; For three transgressions of Edom, and for four, I will not turn away the punishment thereof; because he did pursue his brother with the sword, and did cast off all pity, and his anger did tear perpetually, and he kept his wrath for ever:

12 But I will send a fire upon Teman, which shall devour the palaces of Bozrah.

The Edomites were descendants of Esau.

Genesis 36:1

Now these are the generations of Esau, who is Edom.

Even though the men, Jacob and Esau, eventually made things right with each other, their descendants did not learn from the example set by their fathers. The conflict between Edom and Israel would remain for years to come until one day the Edomites are wiped out, and the last remaining Edomite (Herod the Great) tries to have Christ killed as a baby. But we will look deeper into this when the book on Obadiah comes out. (Shameless plug)!

The next nation that God directs Amos to turn his anger toward is Ammon. Ammon is the result of the incestuous relationship between Lot and his youngest daughter after the destruction of Sodom in Genesis 19.

Amos 1:13

Thus saith the LORD; For three transgressions of the children of Ammon, and for four, I will not turn away the punishment thereof; because they have ripped up the women with child of Gilead, that they might enlarge their border:

14 But I will kindle a fire in the wall of Rabbah, and it shall devour the palaces thereof, with shouting in the day of battle, with a tempest in the day of the whirlwind:

15 And their king shall go into captivity, he and his princes together, saith the LORD.

This judgment on Ammon is an interesting one to me. The mention of Ammon ripping up the women with children is not specifically addressed in the Bible, although it seems to be a reference to Judges chapters 10 and 11. In these chapters Ammon has encamped Gilead. Jepthah has been kicked out by his own people because he is the son of a harlot. The Ammonites attack Gilead and get the better of them. Then the Gileadites go back to Jepthah hat in hand and ask him to lead their army, and God delivers Gilead through Jepthah.

However this was a temporary deliverance because Ammon lives on from that day to be a continual thorn in the side of Israel until just before Israel's destruction. History tells us that Assyria came against Ammon and fulfilled Amos' prophecy against them about 12 years before the fall of Israel.

PERSONAL NOTES

CHAPTER 2

Continued Judgment

As we enter the second chapter, Amos' fiery preaching of God's wrath against other nations continues. Amos has already proclaimed God's judgment against Damascus, Gaza, Tyrus, Edom, and Ammon in the first chapter. Amos has one more enemy of Israel to address before Amos' preaching takes (in the eyes of Israel) a shocking turn.

Amos 2:1

Thus saith the LORD; For three transgressions of Moab, and for four, I will not turn away the punishment thereof; because he burned the bones of the king of Edom into lime:

2 But I will send a fire upon Moab, and it shall devour the palaces of Kerioth: and Moab shall die with tumult, with shouting, and with the sound of the trumpet:

3 And I will cut off the judge from the midst thereof, and will slay all the princes thereof with him, saith the LORD.

Now comes Moab, the illegitimate son of Lot's incestuous relationship with his eldest daughter. Moab is mentioned 151 times in Scripture. They are probably best known in scripture for being the home of Ruth, it lies in the area that is known as Jordan today. Kerioth was the main city in the nation of Moab.

We first read of the Moabites in Genesis 19, when we are told of the birth of Moab, and how he became the father of the Moabites. We really don't know anything about how they grew or developed in the 400 plus years that Israel was in Egypt. But we do know how they treated Israel when they came out of captivity. They were a major thorn in the side of Israel from the very beginning of their journey.

It all started in Numbers 21. Moab had sat back and watched while Israel passes around their boarders. Can you imagine sitting there in your tiny nation, and this group of 3 million plus nomads just slowly walk around the boarders of your country. Israel had sent word to the king of the Amorites, asking permission to pass through their land, but they were rejected. The Bible tells us that the Amorites came out to fight against Israel. All the Israelites wanted to do was pass through the land, but because of the refusal of king Sihon, the Amorites lost the battle and Israel did not just pass through the land, but they now possessed the land.

You may be reading this thinking, *"how is that relevant to the story?"* Well the next chapter of Numbers tells us this.

Numbers 22:1
And the children of Israel set forward, and pitched in the plains of Moab on this side Jordan by Jericho.
2 And Balak the son of Zippor saw all that Israel had done to the Amorites.
3 And Moab was sore afraid of the people, because they were many: and Moab was distressed because of the children of Israel.

Balak, the king of Moab sat back and watched all this unfold between Israel and the Amorites and fear gripped his heart. This is when he reaches out to Balaam to curse the children of Israel. Moab has constantly been a threat, a thorn in the flesh of Israel. And God is announcing His judgment against them!

So we set the scene in chapter 1 with Amos walking into town, and starting a street preaching ministry. He preaches God's judgment against Israel's enemies as the crowds begin to gather and shout Amen. He preaches against the distant cousins of Edom, Ammon, and Moab and the Israelites are worked into a fever pitch as they are in agreement of the justification of God's anger against them. But, at the mentioning of the next target of Amos' preaching, the crowd goes silent, as the blood drains from their face.

A Chilling Realization

Amos 2:4-5

4 Thus saith the LORD; For three transgressions of Judah, and for four, I will not turn away the punishment thereof; because they have despised the law of the LORD, and have not kept his commandments, and their lies caused them to err, after the which their fathers have walked:

5 But I will send a fire upon Judah, and it shall devour the palaces of Jerusalem.

Judah is their goody two shoes brother to the south. At first glance, we might think Israel is happy about God's judgment against Judah, but in the back of Israel's mind they know that if God is upset with Judah, then He is certainly upset with them.

Just look at the reasons God is angry with Judah. They were not threshing innocent people with tools of iron, as Syria did. They did not unjustly deliver up innocent people to Edom like Gaza, or double cross their allies as Tyrus did. What was God's message against Judah? Amos lists three complaints against Judah. They despised the law of the Lord, they have not kept the commandments of God, and their lies have caused them to err in the commandments of God. Judah has had bad kings and good kings. Times of rebellion, and times of Revival. And Israel knows that if God is angry with Judah, although they wouldn't admit it openly, they know that He is certainly upset with them as well!

One thing that we are reminded of in these passages is that God has a great memory. Many of the things that Amos is crying out against here in these first two chapters have happened many, many years ago.

Now that Amos has a captive audience, he begins delivering the message that God sent him with. This is the main reason that he is there.

Israel's sin Uncovered

Amos 2:6-8

6 Thus saith the LORD; For three transgressions of Israel, and for four, I will not turn away the punishment thereof; because they sold the righteous for silver, and the poor for a pair of shoes;

7 That pant after the dust of the earth on the head of the poor, and turn aside the way of the meek: and a man and his father will go in unto the same maid, to profane my holy name:

8 And they lay themselves down upon clothes laid to pledge by every altar, and they drink the wine of the condemned in the house of their god.

God's complaints against Israel can be listed in three main categories; Social Injustice, Spiritual Idolatry, and Sexual Immorality.

Social injustice is a hot topic of our day, but most of what is cried out against on main stream media and social media as social injustice is petty arguments at best. This was a very prosperous time in Israel's history for some, but for others they were still very difficult times. The poor were being sold and traded as if they were nothing more than cattle. The Righteous, those that still wanted to live for God, were looked down upon as old fashioned, rigid, militant. Not willing to accept the "new" ways of worship, the righteous were sold and traded just as the poor were. They had forgotten the commandment of God through Solomon in the book of Proverbs.

Proverbs 14:31

He that oppresseth the poor reproacheth his Maker: but he that honoureth him hath mercy on the poor.

As rich as Solomon was, the poor were never forgotten under his rule. He mentions them thirty-eight times in the book of Proverbs.

God told Israel in the Books of Moses, how he wanted them to conduct business. If a man was in need of a loan, he could go to his brother and borrow what he needed. However, there were rules that God put in place to protect the borrower.

Exodus 22:26-27

26 If thou at all take thy neighbour's raiment to pledge, thou shalt deliver it unto him by that the sun goeth down:

27 For that is his covering only, it is his raiment for his skin: wherein shall he sleep? and it shall come to pass, when he crieth unto me, that I will hear; for I am gracious.

So if a man needed a loan, he would go to his brother and provide his coat for collateral. The lender would hold that coat through the day, but at night the borrower would come back and receive his coat back from the lender. You see this was not just their coat, but it was also their blanket, their covering at night. So, it was the lender's responsibility to give it back at evening time. The next morning, the borrower would return the coat to the lender, and the process would be repeated until the load was paid. Not only that, but if a widow needed to borrow, the lender was not to take a pledge from them at all.

Deuteronomy 24:17

Thou shalt not pervert the judgment of the stranger, nor of the fatherless; nor take a widow's raiment to pledge:

These are laws that God had clearly laid out for his people to protect the borrower from predatory lenders. However, Amos makes it clear that this is a law that was severely violated by Israel. Some might try to claim ignorance to God's command, but God plainly gave the law to all. If they were ignorant of God's law that was their own fault, not God's. Whether they had broken this law through ignorance or defiance, the results are the same, judgment.

So not only were they selling the poor and the righteous, not only were they keeping the coats of the poor that were coming to them for loans, but they were using these coats in their Idolatrous worship. Look at verse eight again;

Amos 2:8

And they lay themselves down upon clothes laid to pledge by every altar, and they drink the wine of the condemned in the house of their god.

They were keeping the coats of the poor, leaving them cold and unprotected at night, just so they could pile them up and make a warm soft bed for them to lay on while they practice their idolatry. Amos said at the end of that verse that they were committing these sins, not in the house of THE God, but in the house of THEIR god. Any thing the Bible calls YOUR god, or THEIR god, is not THE God, and is Idolatry.

This is where the spiritual idolatry comes in. I will not belabor the point here, because Israel is eaten up with this problem, and it is addressed by Amos all through the book. Some might wonder why God would let this happen to His people, but Amos makes it clear that God is keeping track, and this behavior will not go unpunished. Maybe, just maybe, Paul was correct when he said the following;

Galatians 6:7

Be not deceived; God is not mocked: for whatsoever a man soweth, that shall he also reap.

Sexual immorality was ramped in Israel, as it is in any nation or people that forsakes God's law. It is amazing how it is always justified through human reasoning. Fornication is justified as *"making sure we are compatible before marriage."* Adultery is justified with, *"they were not filling my needs."* Homosexuality is justified as, *"an alternative lifestyle."* What God calls sin, is sin! No matter what we say, or how we justify it. We may convince ourselves that our sin is ok, we may convince others that our sin is ok, but we will never convince God!

Look what God has done

Amos 2:9

Yet destroyed I the Amorite before them, whose height was like the height of the cedars, and he was strong as the oaks; yet I destroyed his fruit from above, and his roots from beneath.

Amos shifts gears in verse nine, he goes from telling them God's problem with them to reminding them what God did for them. He brings up the Amorites, A people that were well known to Israel in their early days coming out of Egypt and making their way into the land of Canaan. These were among Israel's fiercest enemies during that period of time. Just look at how Amos describes them in the verse we just read, *"whose height was like the height of the cedars."* But now, they were no longer a people that Israel had to deal with. As a matter of fact, they were no longer around at all. God had certainly destroyed them from the fruit to the Root!

Here is the most amazing part of that story. We cannot point to any one particular battle where Israel wiped them off the face of the map. No doubt Israel would sit and worry and fret, "*how are we going to beat the Amorites this time? Sure, God delivered us last time, but what about now?"* In battle after battle, the strength of the Amorites decreased, and Israel's increased. God delivered them bit by bit until one day Israel looked around and realized, *"Hey, where did all the Amorites go?"* Isn't that what happens in our lives so many times? We worry and fret about this big problem in our lives, sometimes God delivers in a resounding victory, but many times He doesn't. Many times he delivers quietly. How often has problems come, we pray, and we ask the Lord for help until one day, after months of being faithful to God, we realize that we no longer have to deal with that issue that just weeks or months earlier, we didn't know how we would survive it.

Amos 2:10

Also I brought you up from the land of Egypt, and led you forty years through the wilderness, to possess the land of the Amorite.

Have you ever argued with someone, and it is painfully clear that you have the righteous position? You have multiple points to prove you are correct. You lay out your first point, which should be enough to put the issue to rest. But you have so many good points to add, and your second point is just as good as the first, so you throw your second point in with the excitation, *"and another thing!"* That's what Amos has done when he starts verse 10 out with the word, *"Also."* In essence, what Amos is telling them is this. If God delivering you from the

Amorites wasn't good enough. Think about what He did for you when He delivered you from Egypt. How He brought the plagues, changed the heart of Pharaoh, delivered you across the Red Sea, drowned Pharaoh and his army in it, cared for you in the wilderness, provided water, manna, shade, and heat, made your clothes grow with you, and re-soled your shoes while you were asleep. HE'S A GOOD GOD!!!

Amos 2:11

And I raised up of your sons for prophets, and of your young men for Nazarites. Is it not even thus, O ye children of Israel? saith the LORD.

Amos continues on his righteous rant in verse 11. Amos is no longer telling them about the enemy God destroyed, or the captivity He led them out of, but he's reminding them what God did for their families. The greatest gift a parent can have, is to see their children serving God! The apostle John said the following;

3 John 1:4

I have no greater joy than to hear that my children walk in truth.

What a privilege to have God call your children into the ministry, to see them develop a love for the Bible, and desire a relationship with Him! To choose a life of service to God over a life of worldly pleasures.

He also mentions the *"young men for Nazarites."* These are young men who made sacrifices in their lives in order to have a closer and more personal relationship with God! Oh how we need a generation of young people today that want God more than they want the things of this world!

Amos 2:12

But ye gave the Nazarites wine to drink; and commanded the prophets, saying, Prophesy not.

This is human nature at its finest! How often has God given a statute, or a precept. But instead of following that command from God, we find a way to pervert it, to excuse it. *"Well God didn't really mean it that way."* Yes, He did really mean it that way! Isaiah and Amos were prophesying about the same time. We can see that they are dealing with the same cold hearted conditions!

Isaiah 30:10

Which say to the seers, See not; and to the prophets, Prophesy not unto us right things, speak unto us smooth things, prophesy deceits:

What we need in this generation is to start following the Bible, and stop trying to redefine the Bible. This world changes, but God does not! What was sin in Amos' day, is still sin today!

The Breaking Point

Now, I know that God does not have a breaking point, in the way that we think of. But God does have lines, and Israel has crossed them. In this chapter, we've seen God's complaint against Israel, verses 6-8, we've seen a brief explanation of all God has done for them in verses 9-12. Now in the last four verses of the chapter, we see that God has had enough.

Amos 2:13-16

13 Behold, I am pressed under you, as a cart is pressed that is full of sheaves.

14 Therefore the flight shall perish from the swift, and the strong shall not strengthen his force, neither shall the mighty deliver himself:

15 Neither shall he stand that handleth the bow; and he that is swift of foot shall not deliver himself: neither shall he that rideth the horse deliver himself.

16 And he that is courageous among the mighty shall flee away naked in that day, saith the LORD.

So basically God is saying this. I have had it up to here with your sins, your idolatry, and your injustice to your brethren. I delivered you from Egypt, brought you through the Red Sea, and took care of you for forty years in the wilderness. I wiped out the Amorites when you thought that they were too much to handle, I called your sons to be prophets, and gave you young men with a special burden and calling on their hearts and lives. And what did you do? You despised it! You told the prophets not to prophesy. You gave the Nazarites wine to drink, intentionally and deliberately derailing their vow that they made to God! They weren't even tempted to do evil by the world, they were tempted to do evil by the very people of God! No wonder God said in verses 13, I am pressed under you!

It is also no wonder that verse 14 starts out with a *"Therefore."* In other words, get ready! God is about to tell you what is going to happen because of everything he's just said in the previous few verses. Those of you that think you can run fast, you cannot out run the judgment of God. Those of you that think you are strong, your strength will not deliver you when God sends the Assyrians.

He continues in verse 15. To those that think they can shoot a bow, you're no match when God is not on your side. For those of you that pride yourself on your riding skills. There is no horse fast enough to deliver you when God has had enough! And he finishes in verse 16 with those that think they are brave, tough, a mans man. You'll be defeated and naked when God is through with you. We are no match for God friend! Israel should have heeded the warning that Solomon gave to them two hundred years earlier.

Ecclesiastes 12:13

Let us hear the conclusion of the whole matter: Fear God, and keep his commandments: for this is the whole duty of man.

PERSONAL NOTES

CHAPTER 3

A Softer, Gentler Amos

Amos 3:1-2

1 Hear this word that the LORD hath spoken against you, O children of Israel, against the whole family which I brought up from the land of Egypt, saying,

2 You only have I known of all the families of the earth:therefore I will punish you for all your iniquities.

There is no doubt that Amos was a man's man. There is no doubt that Amos was God's man. I mentioned in the first chapter that Amos and Hosea were both prophesying at about the same time, to the same people. However these two men could not be any more different in their personality, and in their delivery. And there is nothing wrong with that! I can imagine Hosea is a man who would cry when he preached, wore his heart on his sleeve. Amos was a man known for making bold statements, and not pulling any punches. God sent Hosea, because he wanted a Hosea. God sent Amos, because he wanted an Amos. That should be a lesson to every young preacher. Preach the word of God clearly, and concisely, but do it according to the personality in which He made you. Don't try to be someone else.

But having said that, in this chapter we can see a slight crack in the tough exterior of Amos. It seems as if Amos takes a deep calm breath, then begins chapter three. Although Amos' primary audience is the northern tribes of Israel, he makes sure to remind them that Judah is not exempt. And I say that because of the statement he makes in verse 1, *"the whole family which I brought up from the land of Egypt."* He wants Judah to know that although Israel is primarily on God's radar right now, God has great expectations for Judah as well.

Verse 2 of chapter 3 is where we see a little bit of Hosea coming through in Amos' preaching. We see it in those first five words, *"You only have I known."* Now, I'm not one who runs to the Greek and Hebrew for every little thing, I believe God preserved His word for us in the King James Bible. But I'm also not one of these that say you should never look at the Greek and Hebrew. There are certainly times when looking to the original language can shed brighter light on the subject at hand. If you look at the fifth word of verse 2, *"known,"* that is a very interesting word.

It comes from the Hebrew word, *Yada*. That is the same word that the word *"Knew"* is translated from in Genesis 4.

Genesis 4:1

And Adam knew Eve his wife; and she conceived, and bare Cain, and said, I have gotten a man from the LORD.

This goes further than just having a general knowledge of someone. This implies an intimate relationship. In other words, God is telling Israel that they are His sweetheart, that He has had a special love for them. He has been faithful to them and them alone. No other nation holds a place in God's heart, like the nation of Israel has. But, they have not reciprocated that love. And because of this, God will bring judgment into their lives.

The Interrogation

From verse 3, to verse 6, Amos asks Israel seven questions. Now these are not legitimate questions that he is looking for answers to. But they are in-fact, rhetorical.

Amos 3:3-6

3 Can two walk together, except they be agreed?

4 Will a lion roar in the forest, when he hath no prey? will a young lion cry out of his den, if he have taken nothing?

5 Can a bird fall in a snare upon the earth, where no gin is for him? shall one take up a snare from the earth, and have taken nothing at all?

6 Shall a trumpet be blown in the city, and the people not be afraid? shall there be evil in a city, and the LORD hath not done it?

We often use verse 3 in application to fellowship with a brother, and that is a good application. However the proper interpretation of this passage is not addressing our relationship with our fellow man, but our fellowship with the Father. The Lord had made it painfully clear to them way back in Leviticus that if they were not willing to walk with Him, then He would not be willing to walk with them!

Leviticus 26:21-23

21 And if ye walk contrary unto me, and will not hearken unto me; I will bring seven times more plagues upon you according to your sins.

22 I will also send wild beasts among you, which shall rob you of your children, and destroy your cattle, and make you few in number; and your high ways shall be desolate.

23 And if ye will not be reformed by me by these things, but will walk contrary unto me; Then will I also walk contrary unto you, and will punish you yet seven times for your sins.

This is not speaking of a loss of salvation, but a loss of fellowship, and discipline coming into their lives.

In verse 4 He asks, *"will a lion roar in the forest, when he hath no prey?"* Essentially God is asking them if they think that He is giving vain threats. God is not in the habit of threatening punishment and never following through with it. He is not the parent that tells their child, *"if you do that again I'm going to spank you."* Then, an hour later, when their child has committed that offense again for the forty-seventh time, the parent still hasn't taken action. God has warned Israel, He has given grace, and He has given space to repent. But now He is telling them that they can rest assured that punishment is coming.

Verse 5 tells us that they have been snared by satan. *"Can a bird fall in a snare upon the earth, where no gin is for him?"* God has warned Israel repeatedly about idolatry, and all other manner of sin, yet they keep stepping into the same mess that the devil sets out for them. If an investor has a winning strategy that continually makes him money, why would he change? If a business man has a model of success that has proven itself true over and over, wouldn't it make sense for him to continue to use that same business model? The devil knows what works on us, so why change tactics when he's found one that works, and works so efficiently?

In verse 6, Amos is likening the warning that he is sounding to the warning a trumpeter would sound from the walls of a city in the face of danger. Imagine living in the walled cities like they lived in during that time. Going about your daily life, buying food in the market place. All of a sudden, you hear the trumpet blast from the wall of the city. It is a blast of warning. Your blood runs cold, because you know that means that there is an invading army approaching with the intent of putting your city under siege. It would strike immediate fear in the hearts of you, and everyone in the city.

But here is the problem. Amos is sounding a warning, Hosea is sounding a warning, Isaiah is sounding a warning, all around the same time. And no one is listening! Imagine yourself back in that same city market. The trumpet sounds, everyone stops, you can hear a pin drop. You make eye contact with a few strangers around you. You all are aware of what the trumpet blast means. Danger is at the gate. Then simultaneously, everyone goes back to what they were doing, conversations resume, just as if nothing has happened. This is what has Amos so dumbfounded! God has spoken, and no ones cares!

God's Man, with God's Message

Amos 3:7

Surely the Lord GOD will do nothing, but he revealeth his secret unto his servants the prophets.

The arrogance of Israel in this verse is amazing. *"Surely the Lord God will do nothing."* They are falling into the mindset that Solomon warned of in Ecclesiastes.

Ecclesiastes 8:11

Because sentence against an evil work is not executed speedily, therefore the heart of the sons of men is fully set in them to do evil.

But in the last half of verse 7 God is saying, *"not so fast Israel. I've told my prophets, Amos, Hosea, and Isaiah, exactly what I'm going to do!"* They did not have the completed scriptures in those days, so God used prophets to deliver his messages. Messages of warning, messages of encouragement, messages of exhortation. Do you know the wonderful thing about this is? In these days we do not need prophets, we have the word of God!

Hebrews 1:1

1 God, who at sundry times and in divers manners spake in time past unto the fathers by the prophets,

2 Hath in these last days spoken unto us by his Son, whom he hath appointed heir of all things, by whom also he made the worlds;

Amos brings up the roaring lion again in verse number 8.

Amos 3:8

The lion hath roared, who will not fear? the Lord GOD hath spoken, who can but prophesy?

Amos is in essence saying this, *"Do you hear what God has said? Did you hear what He's going to do to you? How can you sit there so calm?"* Oh, that is a good question for America today. I guess the reason I love the book of Amos so much is because I see America in this story. God has been good to us, just like He has been to Israel. God has blessed us, just like He had Israel. And how are we responding? Just like Israel did. With Idolatry, and complacency.

But Amos didn't let the verse finish there. He said, *"the Lord God hath spoken, who can but prophesy?"* Amos is basically saying that he is going to do right, regardless of what Israel does. Lord help us to have the same attitude, to live for God in spite of what the world around us is doing!

Amos 3:9

Publish in the palaces at Ashdod, and in the palaces in the land of Egypt, and say, Assemble yourselves upon the mountains of Samaria, and behold the great tumults in the midst thereof, and the oppressed in the midst thereof.

This brings another verse into stark contrast. In II Samuel you have David lamenting the death of Saul. David makes those great and wonderful statements, *"how are the mighty fallen!"* But in the midst of that, David makes another statement. *"Tell it not in Gath, publish it not in the streets of Askelon."* It is intriguing to me that you have David in one verse saying, let's not publish the sins of Saul, and you have Amos in chapter 3 basically saying, let's get everyone together and get the sins of Israel all out in public.

Here is what I believe makes the difference between these two situations. Saul was a terrible king, everyone knew that. David had at least two chances to kill Saul, but he did not. He determined that he was going to let God take care of the Saul problem, and God did! God brought judgment on Saul. He was dealt with swiftly and suddenly. Saul was judged, the problem was over. So David said, *"let's not talk about it anymore. Don't tell it in Gath how God brought judgment on the man that was king over God's people."* The problem in Amos' day is this, they were still in their sins, they were still wrapped up in their idolatry.

God had not yet judged them. So, God through Amos decides the best way to deal with this is to get it all out in the open.

Amos 3:10

For they know not to do right, saith the LORD, who store up violence and robbery in their palaces.

The first statement in this verse amazes me. These were God's people, yet they did not know right from wrong. They knew who God was, they knew of the stories of Egypt, Moses, the Red Sea, the forty years in the wilderness. They knew of the judges, Samuel, Saul, David and Solomon. Yet they did not know what God expected from their lives! Again, the application can certainly be drawn to Americans today. I see so much about God, religion, and the Bible on the internet, on YouTube. And the majority of what is out there is false. This world knows about God, but they don't know what He says. They don't know what He expects from us, and they are perfectly happy with their ignorance.

In that last verse, he makes the statement that they, *"store up violence and robbery in their palaces."* Remember in chapter 2 when they had taken peoples coats as pledges for loans, then not return them at night as God had commanded? God is telling them that since they disobeyed His command, and made their beds in the house of their god (Amos 2:8) that he was going to destroy the source of their pride. He was going to destroy their palaces.

Amos 3:11

Therefore thus saith the Lord GOD; An adversary there shall be even round about the land; and he shall bring down thy strength from thee, and thy palaces shall be spoiled.

Let's fast forward in time a few decades and address the fulfillment of this warning that is given in verse 11. Amos does not give them the specifics on who, when, and where their destruction will come from, however he does get pretty close. But we have the privilege of looking back in history and seeing what has taken place.

Time lines in the Old Testament can be a little difficult to nail down solid. But most historians have Amos prophesying somewhere in the 780's to 750's B.C. I believe it to be about 755B.C. Regardless of when Amos prophesied, we do know exactly when Israel fell.

In the 720's. Hoshea was king over Israel. Assyria was a growing power on the worlds stage, and a big threat to the sovereignty of Israel. Israel had been sending gifts and tribute to Assyria for several years. Hoshea, for what ever reason, thought that he could employ the help of the Egyptians to break the death grip that Assyria had on Israel. Hoshea was so confident that the Egyptians would help him, that he stopped paying tribute to the Assyrians. When Sargon II, king of Assyria, got the 30 day late notice on the tribute payment from Israel, he was not at all happy. Then, he got wind of Hoshea's attempt to reach out to Egypt for help. Assyria then besieged Israel for three years, killing many (we'll see that in chapter 5) and taking the rest captive in 722bc. We read about this in II Kings chapter 17.

This chapter is also where the Samaritans originate from. As you read II Kings 17 you'll see how the king of Assyria brought people (Gentiles) to dwell in the now uninhabited land of Israel. God sent lions among them to kill them. The superstitious nature of the Assyrians assumed that the god's of the land were angry, and sent some of the Israelites back to dwell in the land. They co-mingled with the Gentiles that were there, and produced the Samaritan race of people, that the Jews despised. (See John 4).

This concludes our brief look into the future with the last few paragraphs. We now continue on to see what else Amos has to say to the stunned Israelites.

The Remnant

Amos 3:12

Thus saith the LORD; As the shepherd taketh out of the mouth of the lion two legs, or a piece of an ear; so shall the children of Israel be taken out that dwell in Samaria in the corner of a bed, and in Damascus in a couch.

This is an interesting analogy, and actually describes in detail what we just talked about in the previous paragraph. What Amos is saying in verse 11 is this. A shepherd will not stand idly by and watch his sheep be torn to pieces by a lion, he will step in and fight for him. And although he may not save the life of the sheep, he will not let the lion devour him completely. He may only save a leg, or the piece of an ear, but he will fight for what is his. God said, that Israel is going to be torn to pieces. But He will not let them be completely devoured or eliminated. He will save a remnant of His people!

Amos 3:13

Hear ye, and testify in the house of Jacob, saith the Lord GOD, the God of hosts,

14 That in the day that I shall visit the transgressions of Israel upon him I will also visit the altars of Bethel: and the horns of the altar shall be cut off, and fall to the ground.

15 And I will smite the winter house with the summer house; and the houses of ivory shall perish, and the great houses shall have an end, saith the LORD.

It's bad enough that Israel has disgraced their name among the nations. The Israelites were know as the people of Jehovah, but over the past couple of hundred years they have drug their own name through the mud with their idolatry and pagan practices. But that is not the worse part. Israel not only disgraced their name, but they disgraced the name of the house of God (Bethel). They brought their sin and idolatry into the house of God (we will discuss this in greater detail in the next chapter) and as a result God is having to bring judgment on Bethel.

He says specifically that the *"horns of the altar shall be cut off."* Horns are a representation of power. God is saying that because of all the idolatry and wickedness that has been brought into their worship, the power that this house once had would be no longer.

PERSONAL NOTES

CHAPTER 4

A Word to the Women

Amos 4:1

Hear this word, ye kine of Bashan, that are in the mountain of Samaria, which oppress the poor, which crush the needy, which say to their masters, Bring, and let us drink.

2 The Lord GOD hath sworn by his holiness, that, lo, the days shall come upon you, that he will take you away with hooks, and your posterity with fishhooks.

3 And ye shall go out at the breaches, every cow at that which is before her; and ye shall cast them into the palace, saith the LORD.

Amos comes out swinging in chapter number 4. No moment of sweet remembrance as he did at the beginning of chapter 3, quite the contrary. Amos has cleared his throat, regained his composure, loads both barrels and pulls both triggers at the same time! These first three verses are one flowing thought, addressing one very particular set of individuals.

He starts out, as he did in the previous chapter, with the exclamation, *"Hear this word."* This is now the second time that he has started a chapter out with this statement. So obviously Amos knows that what he has to say is of utmost importance. Then he says, *"Ye Kine of Bashan."* Now look, I am a literalist. I believe that the Bible is to be taken literally, except for the occasions that it is obvious that God is speaking metaphorically. I know people who want to split hairs over whether a passage is meant to be literal, or whether it is meant to be metaphorical. God gave us common sense for a reason. When Jesus said in John 10:9 *"I am the door."* I'm 99.9% sure (ok, I'm 100% sure) that he is speaking metaphorically. Common sense tells us that Jesus is not saying he is a six panel, right-handed interior door. If you and I are carrying on a conversation and I use the phrase *"well I'll be John Brown,"* and you literally think I mean that my name is John Brown and I've been lying to you all these years and my name is not Brad Thompson, then I'm sorry, but you need your head examined! There are many people that want to take a passage that is obviously meant to be taken literal, and turn it into a metaphor. Or vise versa.Thats crazy!

Why do I stress this point? Because of who Amos is addressing in this passage. I do know men who have gotten out in the woods and preached to the animals, (there is nothing wrong with this by the way) but I do not believe that Amos is preaching to the cows (kine) in this passage, but he is preaching to people that he is calling cows. Now, I would assume that this would be blatantly obvious to anyone that is reading this passage, and no further exposition should be needed. But, for the few of you that still need convincing, let's look at the passage further.

First of all, he identifies the location as Bashan. Immediately we see that we have a problem if Amos is speaking literally, because he is in Israel. Bashan is a region east of the Jordan river between mount Hermon and the mountains of Gilead. This place was famous for one thing. Growing healthy, strong, delicious, melt in your mouth cattle.

Do you remember in the book of Numbers chapter 32, the children of Israel were getting ready to cross over Jordan to go into the promise land? The Bible says that the children of Ruben and the children of Gad had *"a very great multitude of cattle."* So, they came to Moses and Eleazar the priest and made a request that they would not have to cross into the promise land. And this is their reason as to why they wanted to stay there, *"...is a land for cattle, and thy servants have cattle."* I'll give you one guess as to the area that this land happen to be a part of. It neighbored the area of Bashan.

Much like the wagyu beef produced in Japan today is considered to be the best in the world, the Bulls of Bashan were the wagyu beef of Israel's day. This area was known for its ability to produce quality live stock. Now, there is American wagyu, but if you want the real thing, the location of where the cows are raised is vitally important. This is why I'm stressing the location of Amos verses the location of the cows of Bashan, they are not in the same zip code (so to speak). Amos is in Israel, but so are the cows that he is addressing. That is evident by his next statement, *"that are in the mountains of Samaria."* So, if he is literally addressing the cows of Bashan he would have to be in Bashan, not Israel. Because Bashan is where the cows are. So, the fact that Amos is in Israel addressing the cows of Bashan means one of two things. Either he is speaking metaphorically, or he is addressing the cows after they are cooked and sitting on a plate, not standing in a pasture. The kine of Bashan were not produced in Israel, they were raised in Bashan. They were consumed in Israel!

With all that being said, I believe that we have made it painfully obvious that Amos is speaking metaphorically and not literally in his addressing of the Kine. But lets beat this dead horse (or cow) for a few more paragraphs while we're here.

He said that these cows *"oppress the poor,"* and they, *"crush the needy."* I know that cows can be oppressive, (you know this if you've ever been chased by one through a pasture) but they are not selective in who they oppress. Cows will chase the rich as well as the poor. But the cows that Amos is addressing in this passage seem to have a particular distain for the poor.

Verse 1 reveals something else that is interesting about these kine, *"which say to their masters."* So if these are actual cows, then we now know the secret why the cows of Bashan were so valuable, they could talk! Ok, I'm done with the sarcasm. But it is obvious that *"cows"* are a metaphor.

So now the question is, who are the cows a metaphor for? Whenever I preach on Amos, I always like to bring out how if Amos lived in our day people would say that he had no tact. Amos was the kind of person that told you what was on his mind whether you liked it or not. Amos was the kind of person that would say yes, if his wife asked him *"doeth this robe maketh me look fat?"* That's just the kind of man that Amos was. I believe that it becomes obvious as we study this text that Amos is addressing the women of Israel.

It is interesting that Amos uses the word *"masters"* when he is talking about who the cows, uh, distinguished ladies, are addressing. This word *"master"* can be interpreted in a few different ways. One of the ways that it can be interpreted is a wife addressing her husband. Notice the progression of the conversation as he addresses these kine of Bashan. First, they are in the mountains of Samaria (we've covered that pretty thoroughly). Secondly, they oppress the poor. Thirdly, they crush the needy. And fourthly, they say to THEIR masters. Now, if he is addressing people who have masters in the sense that we would think of a servant having a master, why would they be the same people that are oppressing the poor or crushing the needy? And what kind of servant makes a demand to their masters? These kine of Bashan are giving demands to their masters! *"Bring, and let us drink."* So taking all this into consideration, and the fact that he uses the word *"her"* in verse 3. It is clear that he is addressing the women of Israel.

Notice again what he says in verse two. That the Lord has sworn on His holiness. I'm reminded here of what God said in the book of Hebrews.

Hebrews 6:13

For when God made promise to Abraham, because he could swear by no greater, he sware by himself,

We see many times in the Bible where God repented, that simply means He changed his mind. But God is making it clear here that there will be no repenting in this situation, there will be no changing of mind. Sure, if they repent God will have mercy. But if they don't, they can rest assured that God will perform everything that He has said that He would.

So, what are the promises that He is expressing here? That these women would be carried away by hooks, and their posterity (children) by fish hooks... Ouch! Why would these promises come to the women specifically? Why not the men? In my estimation, it is a two fold reason. One, because the women ran the house hold, they had a great example of a rebellious spouse a few generations earlier in Jezebel. We see in these verses how they are making demands of their husbands, *"masters."* But the second reason could be because most of the men have been killed.

If you'll remember when we were discussing chapter 3, verse 11, we talked about the three year besiegement of Israel by Assyria, I made a reference to chapter 5 verse 3. He said only ten percent of the population would be left. So, we would surmise that most of those killed would be men. That, I believe, is the main reason that Amos is specifically addressing the women when he describes how they will be carried away into captivity.

As we get into verse 3, Amos tells us even more detail about how they will be carried off. *"And ye shall go out at the breaches."* Picture this. Israel has been besieged by Assyria for three years. It's been a bloody and hard fought battle. Now almost all of the men have been killed, all that are left are mostly the women and the children. The city of Samaria lay in tatters, buildings turned to rubble. Smoke ascending up from fires that have been set by the Assyrian army. These *"big beautiful walls,"* once stood as a symbol of their protection. Over time the people began to place their trust in the walls more than their God, now these walls lie in ruin. There are giant holes in the wall that are a result of the awful battles that have taken place. These women and their children will be lead captive to Assyria right out of their front door, and right through the holes in the walls that stood in front of their beautiful homes.

A Sarcastic Word

Amos 4:4

Come to Bethel, and transgress; at Gilgal multiply transgression; and bring your sacrifices every morning, and your tithes after three years:

We see the sarcasm of Amos coming back in view here in verse 4. We briefly discussed Bethel in the last chapter. If you are reading a commentary on the book of Amos, I'm going to assume you already have a pretty good knowledge of your Bible and how significant Bethel is. I mean, if you are a new convert and your pastor told you to study Amos first, that would seem odd to me.

We know that Bethel means the house of God. But when we get to I Kings 12 Solomon has died. Reoboam has split the Kingdom with his foolish decision to listen to the council of his friends rather than the wisdom of his fathers' councilors. Now Jeroboam is the king of ten of the twelve tribes. But Jeroboam has a problem. He knows that when the feast times come, and the northern tribes start making their way down to Jerusalem to keep the biblically directed feasts, they will remember the commands of God and they will realize how terrible of a decision it was to split from the house of David. They'll make amends, go back to Reoboam and kill Jeroboam. Now,

Jeroboam was not particularly fond of the idea of a pre-mature death, so he devised a plan.

Jeroboam decided to put a golden calf in the north, and one in the south. I Kings says that he made priests of the lowest of the people. It tells us he made a feast that was similar to the feasts that God set up. But instead of worshipping the God of Heaven, they were worshiping the golden calf that Jeroboam had made. And this golden calf in the south was located in Bethel!

When Amos tells them, *"come to Bethel and transgress"* that's exactly what they've been doing for nearly 200 years! So the sarcasm Amos is using is this, *"go ahead and go to Bethel and transgress the commandments of God, because you're going to do it anyway!"*

Let me put this in another way. Growing up did you ever do something that your parents told you not to do? They warned you once, but you just thought that you knew better than they did so you decided to push your luck and try it again. If your parents were anything like mine they may have said something like this. *"Go ahead and do it and see what happens."* In case you're wondering, the *"thing that happened"* was not pleasant. I have the scars to prove it! That is the same tone that Amos is taking with Israel here.

Now, Bethel was mentioned in the previous chapter, but this is the first mention by Amos of Gilgal. What is the significance of Gilgal? In Joshua chapter 4 Israel is crossing the Jordan river into the Promise Land. Gilgal is the first place that the children of Israel come to when they enter the Promised Land. God commands that they take twelve stones out of the river, and make a memorial. In Joshua 4:21-24, God said that there is going to come a day, when their children would ask what the stones mean. And they were to tell their children of all the mighty works that God had done for them. How He dried up the waters of the Jordan river, how He brought them over on dry ground. It was a memorial for their children to learn of the greatness of God, and it was a reminder to the parents to never forget where they came from and what God had done for them. But now they have perverted that memorial.

It seems like it has always been in man's nature to take something that has been sanctified and set apart by God and pervert it into something that God never intended for it to be. We see that in Judah years prior.

When Hezekiah came to the throne of Judah in II Kings 18, he began to clean house! The Bible says that he removed the high places, and cut down the groves. But, then it mentions something interesting. The Bible says that he break into pieces the brazen serpent that Moses made. This is the same brazen serpent that was lifted up in the wilderness in Numbers chapter

21. The same brazen serpent that Jesus referred to in John chapter 3 when he was talking to Nicodemus. But, why in the world would Hezekiah feel the need to destroy this wonderful symbol of God's protection and provision? Because II Kings 18 goes on to tell us that in those days (the days leading up to the kingdom of Hezekiah) that the children of Israel were burning incense to the serpent. They were worshiping the serpent instead of the God that brought deliverance. What's also interesting is the name that Hezekiah gave to the serpent. The Bible says that he called it *"Nehushtan."* It means, *"nothing more than an image of brass."*

So it has always been Israel's habit to take something that God meant for good, and pervert it into something God never intended it to be. By the way, that's not just Israel's habit, but it is just simply human nature.

Before we get too critical of Israel, remember that they were not doing everything wrong. There were some things that Israel was doing right. The last half of verse 4 says *"bring your sacrifices every morning, and your tithes after three years."* This is what they were commanded to do in Numbers.

Numbers 28:3

And thou shalt say unto them, This is the offering made by fire which ye shall offer unto the LORD; two

lambs of the first year without spot day by day, for a continual burnt offering.

4 The one lamb shalt thou offer in the morning, and the other lamb shalt thou offer at even;

So, they were being obedient to this part of the law. They were also doing was was commanded them of the tithes.

Deuteronomy 14:28

At the end of three years thou shalt bring forth all the tithe of thine increase the same year, and shalt lay it up within thy gates:

So they were obedient in some areas, but willfully disobedient in others. Some times we may think that because we are obeying God in one area of life, that means that God will give us a pass in other areas. But God doesn't work that way. He demands full obedience from us! Now I can hear the nay sayers at that statement, *"God doesn't demand perfection."* No, but He does demand obedience. There is a big difference between sinning in a moment of weakness and giving into temptation, then being sorry over that fall and coming to God in repentance verses planning on sinning because in our opinion we've been good in other areas and deserve a hall pass.

Amos 4:5

And offer a sacrifice of thanksgiving with leaven, and proclaim and publish the free offerings: for this liketh you, O ye children of Israel, saith the Lord GOD.

We know that leaven is a type or a picture of sin. So at first glance of this verse it may seem that Amos is sarcastically telling them to offer their sacrifices with sin in their hearts and lives. Now, I may be proven to be wrong on this, but I do not think that is what Amos is saying here. I believe this is something that they are actually doing correctly. Most sacrifices were required to be offered without leaven, but not all.

Leviticus 7:12-13

If he offer it for a thanksgiving, then he shall offer with the sacrifice of thanksgiving unleavened cakes mingled with oil, and unleavened wafers anointed with oil, and cakes mingled with oil, of fine flour, fried.

13 Besides the cakes, he shall offer for his offering leavened bread with the sacrifice of thanksgiving of his peace offerings.

So I believe that Amos is telling them something that they are actually doing correctly. They are offering the thanksgiving sacrifices as they are supposed to. But what about the other offerings? What about the sin offering, what about the trespass offering (Leviticus 5)? This I believe, is the sin that Amos is calling out here. They are picking and choosing which laws and offerings they want to follow, and which ones they are excusing.

Much like the modern church member today they are grateful for the success that they have in life, and they attribute this success to the blessings of God. But if you look at how they got those *"blessings"* and how they live contrary to God's Word, we can easily come to the conclusion that it's just success, and God's hand is not in it. God may allow us to be successful in our ventures in life, but that does not mean that it is a blessing of God. God's blessings are not upon us when we are living contrary to His will. By the same token, God's blessings were not upon Israel, but they were so blinded by their sin that they could not see that they were actually living in rebellion against God.

Look at what else they are doing in verse 5 *"...Proclaim and publish the free offerings..."* Anytime they did something for God, they had to tell everyone. We've all seen the videos on social media of people filming themselves feeding the hungry, or doing something good for someone. Their goal is not to be a help, but to get likes and clicks. This mentality hasn't changed, it just evolved with technology. Israel in their day just couldn't help but brag when they gave a free will offering. They had to *"proclaim and publish"* to everyone how good of a person they are.

But notice how he closes that verse out…*"for this liketh you."* God said, this is who you are, this is just like you to do something like this!

Grabbing their Attention

In verses 6 - 11 Amos catalogs everything that God has done to get their attention. But what is interesting, is that everything Amos tells them that God has done, God warned them in Deuteronomy that he was going to do this.

The first 14 verses of Deuteronomy 28 God promises blessings to Israel if they will obey Him. Ten times some variation of the word blessed is used. He tells them in verse in 7 that God will cause their enemies to fear them. In Verse 9 He tells them that He will establish them as a holy people. In verse 10 He tells them that all the people of the earth will be afraid of them. Verse 11 He promises that they will be plenteous in goods. Verse 12 God tells them that they will be the lenders and not the borrowers. All these blessings are promised in the first 14 verses.

But all those blessings are conditional. Four different times he makes sure they know that. In verses 1,2,9, and 13 he emphasizes the word IF. If they are obedient, then God will bless them. The blessings of God were conditional on them being obedient to God.

But when you get to verse 15 of Deuteronomy 28, God starts telling them everything that He will do to them if they are not obedient.

Now getting back to Amos 4, God lists five different things that He has done to get Israel's attention. It is interesting that he points out five things. We know that five is the number of grace, but it has a dual meaning, it is also the number of death. In other words, there are blessings if they obey God, but there is death if they do not!

Notice the first thing that Amos mentions.

Amos 4:6

And I also have given you cleanness of teeth in all your cities, and want of bread in all your places: yet have ye not returned unto me, saith the LORD.

You may be asking yourself, what does good dental hygiene have to do with God judging Israel? Well nothing, but it is easy to keep your teeth clean when you are not eating anything. The *"cleanness of teeth"* that Amos is telling them about is famine that God has sent to them.

However, God told them hundreds of years before that this would be a punishment for not obeying Him.

Deuteronomy 28:51

And he shall eat the fruit of thy cattle, and the fruit of thy land, until thou be destroyed: which also shall not leave thee either corn, wine, or oil, or the increase of thy kine, or flocks of thy sheep, until he have destroyed thee.

Amos reminds them that God has sent drought their way.

Amos 4:7

And also I have withholden the rain from you, when there were yet three months to the harvest: and I caused it to rain upon one city, and caused it not to rain upon another city: one piece was rained upon, and the piece whereupon it rained not withered.

8 So two or three cities wandered unto one city, to drink water; but they were not satisfied: yet have ye not returned unto me, saith the LORD.

As in the case with the famine, God told them hundreds of years prior that this would be the case.

Deuteronomy 28:24

The LORD shall make the rain of thy land powder and dust: from heaven shall it come down upon thee, until thou be destroyed.

The next curse that Amos tells them about is the blasting and mildew. Basically he is telling them that no matter how green their thumb is, they will not even be able to grow weeds when they are living in rebellion.

Amos 4:9

I have smitten you with blasting and mildew: when your gardens and your vineyards and your fig trees and your olive trees increased, the palmerworm devoured them: yet have ye not returned unto me, saith the LORD.

Again, there is a reference in Deuteronomy that warned them of this happening.

Deuteronomy 28:22

The LORD shall smite thee with a consumption, and with a fever, and with an inflammation, and with an extreme burning, and with the sword, and with blasting, and with mildew; and they shall pursue thee until thou perish.

He tells them, *"hey, you know that pestilence that you had to deal with? That wasn't just a natural phenomenon."* Amos makes sure they know that it was God that did that.

Amos 4:10

I have sent among you the pestilence after the manner of Egypt: your young men have I slain with the sword, and have taken away your horses; and I have made the stink of your camps to come up unto your nostrils: yet have ye not returned unto me, saith the LORD.

But again, we see the warning in Deuteronomy God gives that He would do this years before.

Deuteronomy 28:21

The LORD shall make the pestilence cleave unto thee, until he have consumed thee from off the land, whither thou goest to possess it.

And lastly Amos tells them that God has pour out His wrath on them because of their rebellion and idolatry.

Amos 4:11

I have overthrown some of you, as God overthrew Sodom and Gomorrah, and ye were as a firebrand

plucked out of the burning: yet have ye not returned unto me, saith the LORD.

The corresponding verse from Deuteronomy to Amos 4:11 is as follows;

Deuteronomy 28:25

The LORD shall cause thee to be smitten before thine enemies: thou shalt go out one way against them, and flee seven ways before them: and shalt be removed into all the kingdoms of the earth.

So in all five of these instances that God has brought into their lives, the famine in verse 6, the drought in verses 7 and 8, the loss of crops in verse 9, the pestilence in verse 10, and the destruction in verse 11, God warned them years in advance right before they ever entered the Promised Land that He would bring all these things into their lives if they would not live for Him.

God is a just God, He is a fair God. He lets us know up front the expectations that He has for us, the blessings that will come if we follow Him, and the consequences if we do not!

Everything that God brought into their lives, everything that He lists in these verses was not because God is cruel, mean, or vindictive. His only goal was to get the children of Israel to return to Him. We know this because of how he ends each verse. *"Yet have ye not returned unto me, saith the LORD."*

Amos 4:12

Therefore thus will I do unto thee, O Israel: and because I will do this unto thee, prepare to meet thy God, O Israel.

Notice the finality in the tone of Amos. There is no *"or else,"* there is no olive branch extension. They have had two hundred years of that. Now, it is just judgment. The word *"Therefore"* puts a bow on the announcement of their punishment. In verses 6-11 God logs all of His attempts to get their attention. They did not repent after the famine, they did not repent after the drought, or after the rotting of their crops. They had no remorse for their sins, nor any realization of their wrong doings even after God sent the pestilence and the destruction.

Notice the weight of his statements in this verse. *"Thus will I do,"* and *"because I will do this,"* leads us to the declaration, *"prepare to meet thy God."* This is inevitability, this is finality! Yet even with this declaration of in-escapable punishment, knowing the grace of God, we know that even now had they repented and turned to God, that He would have forgiven them.

We see that kind of grace from God exhibited to the Ninevites one hundred years earlier. The very people who God is using now to destroy Israel for their rebellion. When Jonah was preaching against Nineveh, there was no hope, no path of reconciliation in his message. *"Yet forty days and Nineveh shall be overthrown."* However, the Bible says that the people of Nineveh believed God, they repented, put on sack cloth and ashes, and they made this statement, *"who can tell if God will turn..."* We know that God did turn because of their humility, and repentant heart!

How sad it is, when this world exercises more faith in God than the very children of God do! How cold, hard, and indifferent must Israel have been to hear this verdict from Amos, and carry on their lives, business as usual!

Amos 4:13

For, lo, he that formeth the mountains, and createth the wind, and declareth unto man what is his thought, that maketh the morning darkness, and treadeth upon the high places of the earth, The LORD, The God of hosts, is his name.

At the end of verse 12, Amos tells them to prepare to meet their God. Just in case they've forgotten (and judging by the way that they've been living, they have), God reminds them in the last verse of this chapter of exactly who their God is!

Amos declares four things about God to Israel. By telling Israel that God created the mountains and the wind, he is declaring the power of God. We see the perception of God in that he knows their very thoughts. We see the presence of God, *"he treadeth upon the high places."* And we see the person of God in Amos' introduction of Him *"The LORD, The God of hosts, is his name."*

Here again, we see the sarcasm of Amos. They know who God is, they need no introduction, but they don't live like they know Him. So, Amos says; *"hey, you've been living like God is a pushover, like His laws are a suggestion, and not a command. Well, let me introduce you to the God that you claim to serve!"* There are a lot of people in this world, that know of God. And because they know of God, they think that they know God. But those are two completely different situations!

PERSONAL NOTES

CHAPTER 5

The Virgin of Israel?

Amos 5:1-3

Hear ye this word which I take up against you, even a lamentation, O house of Israel.

2 The virgin of Israel is fallen; she shall no more rise: she is forsaken upon her land; there is none to raise her up.

3 For thus saith the Lord GOD; The city that went out by a thousand shall leave an hundred, and that which went forth by an hundred shall leave ten, to the house of Israel.

This is the third chapter in a row that starts out with some variation of the phrase, *"Hear this word."* Someone once said that God does not repeat Himself because He cannot think of anything better to say. We should listen the first time God speaks. When God repeats something a second time, it's a reminder to listen. When God repeats Himself a third time, we'd better heed earnestly because we are obviously missing the point that He is trying to get across!

In this chapter, as in chapter 3, we see the emotion of Amos. Not in an outpouring of touchy feely love, but we see the sorrow over what could have been. We know this from the use of the 13th word in the verse, *"lamentation."* Someone said that a lamentation was accompanied with the beating of the breast. Webster described it as an expression of sorrow or the act of bewailing. Israel could have done great things for God had they only listened to Him, but they chose the *"pleasure of sin for a season"* over obedience to God. Sadly, that is the case among most church members today. (Did I even need to make that application)?

On the outset it would seem that Amos made a mistake in verse 2. As he addresses them as *"the virgin of Israel..."* obviously he is not talking about a physical virgin but a spiritual virgin. And obviously, Israel is not pure in their spiritual lives, else there would be no need for Amos to preach against their sins. So, they are anything but spiritual virgins. But he is not addressing Israel as what they are, but as what God sees them to be! Even though they are in rebellion against God, they are still His people. If you haven't made the application yet in your mind, let me help you. Those of us that are saved, don't always live as we should, and there are time when God has to bring judgments into our lives. But even in those times of rebellion and sin against Him, even when He has to bring discipline into our lives, He doesn't see us as lost sinners! But He still sees us as His children! Hallelujah!

Now, it would be a great story of redemption and restoration had they heeded the warning. But as we well know, they did not. Amos goes on to say that this fair virgin that God loves so much has fallen. And not only has she fallen, but she has no hope of recovery, "*she shall no more rise.*" Now in case there is someone reading this that is leaning toward the teachings of replacement theology. Amos doesn't mean that God is done with Israel for all of eternity. It simply means that these people, these particular individuals that are being addressed, will never see freedom again.

In the previous chapter we saw a lot of incredible fulfillments of Moses' warnings from Deuteronomy chapter 28. And we see another one still here.

Deuteronomy 28:62

And ye shall be left few in number, whereas ye were as the stars of heaven for multitude; because thou wouldest not obey the voice of the LORD thy God.

It would be bad enough if Israel were just going to be taken into captivity. But I'm not sure that that is even the worse part. God said that ninety percent of them would be killed in the battle that preceded their captivity. Look at verse 3 again.

Amos 5:3

For thus saith the Lord GOD; The city that went out by a thousand shall leave an hundred, and that which went forth by an hundred shall leave ten, to the house of Israel.

Now I grew up in the era before common core math. So using basic math skills (a hundred left out of a thousand, and ten being left out of one hundred) I see only ten percent of the people in Israel actually surviving the siege of Assyria and go into captivity. The rest are killed in battle. That is a chilling number! Do you remember how we discussed in chapter 3 that Assyria besieged Israel for three years before they actually led them into captivity? There is always a steep price to pay in rejecting God's commandments. Our God is very patient and long-suffering, but just as you and I, God has a limit to his patience. Israel had been getting away with their sins for two hundred years. This lulled them into an attitude of apathy. They mistook God's patience for acceptance. Never ever look at the long-suffering of God in your life and think that God is going to let you get away with your sins. He has never let anyone before, and He will not start with you and me!

Seek the Lord

Amos 5:4

For thus saith the LORD unto the house of Israel, Seek ye me, and ye shall live:

This is the first use of the word *"seek"* in this chapter. As a matter of fact, the word is used five times! Let's just take a brief pause from the study to consider something. Numbers are important in the Bible. You cannot build doctrine on numbers, but they do have their significance. I heard a preacher say once that numbers are God's watermark. Years ago when you would get a paycheck from your employer (it's all direct deposited now) it would have a watermark, something that would be difficult for counterfeiters to duplicate. Thus assuring the bank that the check was authentic. That's what numbers do in the Bible. Because when we see how numbers line up in the Bible, we just have to stand back, smile, and shake our heads in awe, because there is no way that man could do all that!

Getting back to this number five. It is interesting that in chapter one the phrase *"thus saith the Lord"* is used five times. In Chapter four, there are five disasters God brings into the life of Israel to get their attention. And in chapter five, the word *"seek"* is used five times. Five is most often associated with grace, but the number (as with many things in the Bible) has a dual meaning. The number five can also mean death. That is very fitting. God is offering grace to Israel if they repent, but grace rejected brings death!

So the admonition is clear. Seek the Lord! That rings true in any area of our lives. Seek the Lord. I heard someone say once that if you are actively seeking God's will for your life, He will not let you miss it! I guess Matthew knew what he was talking about!

Matthew 6:33
But seek ye first the kingdom of God, and his righteousness; and all these things shall be added unto you.

Amos 5:5
But seek not Bethel, nor enter into Gilgal, and pass not to Beersheba: for Gilgal shall surely go into captivity, and Bethel shall come to nought.

This is the third time that Amos had mentioned Bethel, and he will mention Bethel four more times before the book is over. Every time he talks about Bethel, it has been in a negative connotation. You see, these Israelites were steeped in their idolatry and their wickedness. But they thought that if they could put a spiritual spin on what they were doing, then everything would be ok. Amos has already told us how Bethel has been corrupted, yet they were still hanging on to Bethel as their "saving grace". Like many people today, they want to mix the things of the world, their idolatry, their wicked music, worldly lifestyle, and call it liberty. But when you ask them about their relationship with Christ, they point to their involvement with their worldly church as if that makes everything ok. But God is saying don't seek Bethel, don't seek after those things that look good, that have a spiritual look and feel to it, but in reality it is dripping with carnality and idolatry.

Amos also mentions Gilgal and Beersheba in this verse. Just as with Bethel, we have already covered Gilgal and the significance of it. But what about Beersheba? Beersheba is first mentioned in Genesis 21 when Abraham sends Hagar away. The Bible says that she *"wanders in the wilderness of Beersheba,"* verse 14. Hagar wandered around until she had ran out of water that Abraham had given her. She set her son down, walked away, and sat down. She did not want to witness the death of her son. But then God calls Hagar, and shows her a well of water. So, the first time we see Beersheba, it has to do with water, refreshment, it is a picture of revival.

Beersheba is mentioned again in chapter 26 when Issac was walking through the land, digging wells everywhere. He finally comes to Beersheba in verse 23. And the Lord appeared unto him. Now I don't know about you, but if I had been Issac, and I came across a place where God spoke to me, I think I'd park there for a while. And that is exactly what Issac does! As you continue reading in that passage of Genesis 26 you'll see that the exclamation is made in verse 32 *"we have found water!"* This is the third mention of Beersheba in scripture, and in all three times it is associated with water. This is a picture of the presence and the power of God! Oh how our hearts desire should want to be in the presence of almighty God! Jesus said;

Matthew 5:6
Blessed are they which do hunger and thirst after righteousness: for they shall be filled.

Isaiah said;

Isaiah 44:3
For I will pour water upon him that is thirsty, and floods upon the dry ground: I will pour my spirit upon thy seed, and my blessing upon thine offspring:

Oh, that the child of God would hunger and thirst after Him! That we would seek Him above all else!

HoweverIt was not long until Beersheba too was corrupted. We learn in I Samuel that the sons of Samuel were wicked men. And in chapter 8 verse 2 the Bible tells us that these two corrupt men, Joel and Abiah, were judges in Beersheba.

So, Bethel was known as the House of God, Gilgal was known as a place of remembrance about God, and Beersheba was known as a place of the presence of God. All three of these places once were known as holy places. A place to meet with God, a place of remembrance of God but now, they are so corrupted that Amos has to issue a stark warning against them. Notice how Amos tells us to avoid these places. He said do not seek, or enter, or pass by. In essence, Amos is saying don't look for these places, don't go into these places, don't even get close to these places! He doesn't just leave us there, but he tells us exactly why he is giving the warning. Because God is going to judge them for their sins, *"Gilgal shall surely go into captivity, and Bethel shall come to nought."*

Amos 5:6

Seek the LORD, and ye shall live; lest he break out like fire in the house of Joseph, and devour it, and there be none to quench it in Bethel.

The second admonition in two verses to seek after God! Remember what we said earlier about God repeating Himself? We may get on the bad side of people today, and they can make our lives miserable. We may get on the bad side of the devil, and let me say that as a Christian if we aren't on the bad side of the devil we are doing something wrong, but when we are, he can certainly make life difficult for us. But aren't you glad that when we do get in those bad situations, we have a

Comforter that we can run to. We have an advocate to go to bat for us. However, being on the bad side of your fellow man, or being on the bad side of the devil, is nothing compared to being on the bad side of God! There is nowhere left to run to! Amos said that they will not find help, not even at the house of God.

Amos 5:7

Ye who turn judgment to wormwood, and leave off righteousness in the earth,

We have already seen in chapter 2 how Israel were mistreating the poor among them. Now, Amos is giving us a little more insight into that problem. Notice the *"ye"* here. With that word we know that He is talking about Israel. The theme of this book of Amos is God's coming judgement against Israel. Given that theme it would be easy to think that anytime we see the word judgment, that it is referring to God's judgment against Israel. But that is not what this judgment is referring to. It is referring to Israel's judgments against others.

In other words, Amos is speaking to their unfair justice system. No, Amos is not talking to America here, he's talking to Israel. Wormwood is something that is bitter. Amos is making the application that their injustice is bitterness to the poor and the righteous. When judgment is exercised without righteousness, it always ends in bitterness.

Amos 5:8

Seek him that maketh the seven stars and Orion, and turneth the shadow of death into the morning, and maketh the day dark with night: that calleth for the waters of the sea, and poureth them out upon the face of the earth: The LORD is his name:

The first couple of admonishments in this chapter are to seek after the presence of God. Not just the appearance of the presence of God, but here he is reminding them to seek after the God that is all powerful. Amos is reminding them about this God that they refuse to take serious, this God that they are playing games with. He is reminding them just how incredibly powerful and marvelous this God is! Amos is reminding them that they don't serve the powerless gods of the Philistines, or the graven images of their surrounding nations, but they are serving the God that created the universe. Now yes, they were participating in the feasts, they were keeping the sacrifices. They had the formality of the law, but they did not have the God of the law. They were not embracing the Spirit of the Law. In fact they were so far gone that this is the second time in the book that Amos has felt the need to reintroduce them to Him. *"the LORD is His name."*

Amos 5:9

That strengtheneth the spoiled against the strong, so that the spoiled shall come against the fortress.

God is giving Israel a warning. They may think that they have gotten away with unjust judgments against the poor, the righteous, the needy. But when Amos says that God *"strengtheneth the spoiled,"* he is saying that God will advocate for those that have been spoiled by the corrupt in Israel. He is saying that God will strengthen those that have been wronged and oppressed. In the last half of verse 9 he is telling them not only will He advocate for them, not only will He strengthen them, but He will avenge them.

10 They hate him that rebuketh in the gate, and they abhor him that speaketh uprightly.

In our day, business and legal affairs are usually handled *"down town."* That's where our court houses are, that's where the majority of banks and Fortune 500 businesses are located. But, in Bible times, the city gate (the outskirts) is where business was conducted, and where legal affairs were dealt with.

Amos is saying that in the rare situation there was an uncorrupted judge, that there was someone who was advocating for justice and following God's law. These men were despised, they were shouted down, they were not tolerated. Israel would rather have unrighteousness than righteousness.

They would rather make their gains by their own corrupt means rather than by God's blessings.

Amos 5:11

Forasmuch therefore as your treading is upon the poor, and ye take from him burdens of wheat: ye have built houses of hewn stone, but ye shall not dwell in them; ye have planted pleasant vineyards, but ye shall not drink wine of them.

12 For I know your manifold transgressions and your mighty sins: they afflict the just, they take a bribe, and they turn aside the poor in the gate from their right.

God's declaration in verse 11 is a culmination of everything that He has told them in the last couple of verses. They despised the poor, they hate righteous judgment, they shout down anyone who would dare speak out against evil, they refuse to follow the commandments of God. So God tells them in verse 11 that they will not get to enjoy the fruits of their labor. The Bible tells us that God never changes, He is perpetually the same. Even though we do not read about the reality of there being *"pleasure in sin for a season,"* until Hebrews chapter 11, we can clearly see the principals of that teaching being announced here by Amos. They've made their living by dishonest means for years, but that is quickly coming to an end.

Amos 5:13

Therefore the prudent shall keep silence in that time; for it is an evil time.

Now, there may be some that would take this verse and say, *"see, we should not speak out against sin. We should just keep our mouth shut and let God deal with it."* But I do not believe that is what this verse is teaching at all.

Notice the time that the prudent are keeping silent in. It is not the time before God's judgment falls, but it is the time after God's judgment falls. God is teaching Israel a lesson in character. Israel couldn't help but boast about their success, they would no doubt brag to each other about their unfair business practices and how they cheated another unsuspecting victim out of their hard earned money. Now just in case you think that I'm reading too much into this story, compare this with what Amos says later in the book.

Amos 8:4

Hear this, O ye that swallow up the needy, even to make the poor of the land to fail,

5 Saying, When will the new moon be gone, that we may sell corn? and the sabbath, that we may set forth wheat, making the ephah small, and the shekel great, and falsifying the balances by deceit?

6 That we may buy the poor for silver, and the needy for a pair of shoes; yea, and sell the refuse of the wheat?

It was common practice for Israel to boast and brag about their unsavory business practices. But the difference between them and the prudent is this, when judgment comes against the unjust of Israel the prudent will not be bragging, they will not be rejoicing. They will not be telling everyone, *"They got what they deserved."* They are not rejoicing in the downfall of those that did them wrong. They are sober, they are somber, because they realize that if not for the grace of God, they would be in the exact same spot as the rest of Israel.

Amos 5:14

Seek good, and not evil, that ye may live: and so the LORD, the God of hosts, shall be with you, as ye have spoken.

15 Hate the evil, and love the good, and establish judgment in the gate: it may be that the LORD God of hosts will be gracious unto the remnant of Joseph.

This is the fifth and final admonition in this chapter to seek God. Not the semblance of God *"Seek not bethel"* but to seek Him. There is always room for grace if we will but repent! Even after these verses of hard rebuke from Amos here in chapter 5, he wants to make it clear that if they just turn from their wicked ways, God would have mercy.

Amos is addressing Israel's problem in verse 15. Israel loved the evil, and hated the good all while trying to justify their deeds by claiming that the evil was good! Then he tells them to establish judgment in the gate. He is telling them to stop with the kangaroo courts, and get back to dealing out judgments that are according to God's law, according to righteousness.

Amos 5:16

Therefore the LORD, the God of hosts, the Lord, saith thus; Wailing shall be in all streets; and they shall say in all the highways, Alas! alas! and they shall call the husbandman to mourning, and such as are skilful of lamentation to wailing.

17 And in all vineyards shall be wailing: for I will pass through thee, saith the LORD.

This is the third verse in a row that Amos addresses God in very specific and very different names. In verse 14 Amos says, *"the LORD, the God of hosts."* Any time you see that word LORD in all capital letters in the King James Bible, that is translated from the name Jehovah.

Then he mentions, *"The God of hosts."* The God of armies, or the God of war. There are a lot of names of God in the

Bible that Amos could have used to address God to the children of Israel. Out of all the names in the Old Testament for God, this is not the name you want your prophets to be using when he is talking about how God is going to deal with you!

Amos uses both of these names, in verses 14, 15, and 16. But in verse 16 Amos throws another name of God into the mix. Not LORD, but Lord. The variation in the capitalization of the name indicates the reference to a different root name. This name used here is Adonai, or Master, Sovereign.

Keep in mind that they are a minimum of 25 years away from these events happening. Amos is able to tell them in great detail what they are going to experience, not because there is something special about Amos, but because of the God he serves.

We've already seen in our study how the city will be besieged for 3 years. Imagine the terror of living within a city that your enemy has surrounded for this extended period of time! The skirmishes that would randomly break out, the men of Israel killed in battle, and every time Israel loses just a little more ground. Every time there is another funeral. The starvation and the thirst that is ramped in the city because the supply lines have been cut off, or at the least greatly reduced.

We read at the beginning of this chapter how Amos tells them that only ten percent of the population would even survive to go into captivity.

When we consider all this, no wonder the mourning Amos tells of in verse 16 and 17 is so terrible, so widespread.

Amos 5:18

Woe unto you that desire the day of the LORD! to what end is it for you? the day of the LORD is darkness, and not light.

19 As if a man did flee from a lion, and a bear met him; or went into the house, and leaned his hand on the wall, and a serpent bit him.

20 Shall not the day of the LORD be darkness, and not light?even very dark, and no brightness in it?

Now this subject of *"the day of the Lord"* can be a touchy subject to say the least. I know a lot of good men that differ on exactly what it means. I don't know that anyone can say dogmatically that they have it figured out. So if I say something in the next few paragraphs that you do not agree with, just know that this is what I believe about the day of the Lord based off of the understanding that I have of the subject. But even though we may differ on exactly when the day of the Lord begins, or what it encompasses, let's not get disagreeable. It could be that we are both wrong!

I know of some men who believe that this is a literal 24 hour day. I do not agree with this assessment. Just as we say that we *"live in the day of the cell phone,"* or *"we no longer live in the day of the horse and buggy,"* both of these statements do not refer to a 24 hour day, but a period of time when the cell phone or the horse and buggy reigned supreme. In the same way I believe that the day of the Lord refers to a period of time. More specifically, the end times. Does not the Bible say;

2 Peter 3:8

But, beloved, be not ignorant of this one thing, that one day is with the Lord as a thousand years, and a thousand years as one day.

I believe that the *"day of the Lord"* begins with the rapture of the church, and continues on through the millennial reign of Christ.

The day of the Lord is referred to seventeen times in the Old Testament, and 4 times in the New Testament. So even as misunderstood as the day of the Lord is in our day, you can imagine that it was even more confusing in Amos' day. (Amos' day not being a 24 hour period, but a period of time in which Amos prophesied. See what I did there)?

Now, having stirred up that controversy, let's get back to the text at hand. Apparently these people were going around stating that they were looking forward to the day of the Lord. Amos just looks at them and asks, *"what do you think you have to look forward to?"* We've already cataloged how wickedly and unjustly that Israel was living. Yet they look at the day of the Lord as if it were a time that God would vindicate them and eliminate their enemies when they themselves are living in such a way that violates the scriptures.

Amos goes on to tell them in verse 19, that Israel looking forward to God coming back was like trying to escape one wild beast only to get torn to shreds by another. Or escaping some danger by entering into their house, a place of safety and security, only to lean against the wall and be bitten by a serpent.

They were looking for the day of the Lord as an escape from their troubles, but Amos said that because of the rebellion and idolatry that they have been living in, the day of the Lord is going to be way worse than the troubles that they are facing from their enemies.

Amos 5:21

I hate, I despise your feast days, and I will not smell in your solemn assemblies.

22 Though ye offer me burnt offerings and your meat offerings, I will not accept them: neither will I regard the peace offerings of your fat beasts.

Verse 21 has always amazed me. We discussed in chapter 4, how Jeroboam brought idolatry into Bethel. One thing that we didn't talk about is how he also set up feasts to resemble the ones that God commanded them to keep.

1 Kings 12:32

And Jeroboam ordained a feast in the eighth month, on the fifteenth day of the month, like unto the feast that is in Judah, and he offered upon the altar. So did he in Bethel, sacrificing unto the calves that he had made: and he placed in Bethel the priests of the high places which he had made.

33 So he offered upon the altar which he had made in Bethel the fifteenth day of the eighth month, even in the month which he had devised of his own heart; and ordained a feast unto the children of Israel: and he offered upon the altar, and burnt incense.

Jeroboam made a feast to his images just like the ones that God ordained them to keep in Jerusalem. These were not God ordained feasts, they were Jeroboam ordained. These feasts looked like, smelled like, and sounded like the real feasts. They took place on the same day as the real feasts, but it was pagan worship, it was idolatry. Now they have been keeping these feast for over two hundred years, and God cannot stand it! It has always struck me how He starts out with *"I hate,"* and if that was not emphasis enough, He pauses, and doubles down, *"I despise your feast days."*

We already mentioned how the city was besieged for three years by the Assyrians, killing 90% of the population, leaving only 10% to go into Assyrian captivity. But what happened after they went into captivity? If I gave you all the verses here that I wanted to, I would pretty much have to put the whole chapter of II Kings 17 in this book. So I'll summarize, and you can go and read it later.

In II Kings 17 we have the record of Israel falling at the hand of the Assyrian army. The Bible tells us again in that chapter how God tried to reason with Israel. But the Bible says in verse 14 that they would not hear. They hardened their necks. So they went into captivity. The Assyrians did not want to leave the land empty and vacant. So II Kings 17:24 tells us that they brought men in from Babylon, from Cuthah, and from Ava to occupy the land.

II Kings 17:25 says how God sent lions into the land to devour the people. The Assyrians said, *"it's because the God of the land is angry."* They had no idea just how correct they were.

So the Assyrian's solution was to send one of the priests of Israel back to teach the Gentiles about their God. Now this is one of the very priests that just went into captivity for not following the law of God, so he was about as effective as you would suppose him to be in teaching others about the God of Heaven.

There were some Israeli stragglers left in the land, and it was these stragglers that co mingled with the Gentiles that were brought in and started the race of half breeds known as the Samaritans. As a matter of fact, the first time we see the word Samaritans used is in this chapter in verse 29.

Keep in mind that we are talking about God hating and despising their feast days. Let's quickly recap the progression of their slide from worshipping God to worshipping idols.

In I Kings 12 the kingdom splits. Jeroboam introduces idol worship into Israel telling them that they no longer have to go to Jerusalem for the feasts, but they can stay right there in Bethel and worship the golden calf. Then in II Kings 17, about 200 years later, we find that they go into captivity over their rebellion and idolatrous worship. This is when some of the Israelites co mingle with the gentiles and start the Samaritan race.

Now fast forward 700 years to John chapter 4. The woman at the well, a Samaritan, a descendant of the Israeli Gentile mix of II Kings 17, is still confused about worship.

John 4:20

Our fathers worshipped in this mountain; and ye say, that in Jerusalem is the place where men ought to worship.

This ties right back to I Kings 12 when Jeroboam told them not to go to Jerusalem but stay there in Bethel and worship. They are still confused about the proper way to worship God!

Look what Jesus tells her.

John 4:22

Ye worship ye know not what: we know what we worship: for salvation is of the Jews.

You cannot tell me that the way we worship God is not important! Sadly this is what is wrong with modern churches today. They are worshipping, but they have no idea what they are worshiping. Oh, they call him Jesus, but they are worshipping in such a manner that brings dishonor to Him. Their *"worship"* is sensual, mixing the holy and the profane (Ezekiel 22:26), and it is in direct disobedience to God. But the idea has been so ingrained into them by this modern society, that God will accept anything in anyway, that they have no idea that their *"worship"* is a disgusting smell in the nostrils of God.

Amos 5:23

Take thou away from me the noise of thy songs; for I will not hear the melody of thy viols.

There is so much I could say about music here, but this is not a book on Christian music. However I will say this. So much of what is sung today in churches is either not God honoring, or comes from a source that is rooted in paganism and New Age. Music was created to bring glory to God, it should come from a pure heart, and sung with that same sincerity.

Keep in mind, in their idolatrous worship that they were practicing during Amos' day, they were doing it as if they were worshiping the God of heaven. Now the rulers and the priests, the ones who set the idolatry into motion, they knew well what they were doing. The Bible tells us clearly that the kings of Israel were wicked. The Bible tells us the same of the priests.

1 Kings 12:31

And he made an house of high places, and made priests of the lowest of the people, which were not of the sons of Levi.

Average people on the street, were worshiping as they were instructed to do by the rulers, and by the priests. They did not know that what they were doing was not acceptable to God.

Now here comes this crazy country bumpkin from the land of Tekoa telling them that their worship is unacceptable to

God. How do you think they reacted when Amos told them that their worship was based in idolatry? The same way people react today when you try to show them how this modern worship music (I'm looking at you Bethel and Hillsong) comes from paganism!

Amos 5:24

But let judgment run down as waters, and righteousness as a mighty stream.

So, because of their hard heartedness, their unwillingness to listen to Amos' warning, and their indifference to the laws of God, Amos' answer is this. Judgment is coming! It will flow as water, it will be all consuming. Why you ask? Because God is vindictive? Because God wants to see them suffer? No! So righteousness can prevail!

Amos 5:25

Have ye offered unto me sacrifices and offerings in the wilderness forty years, O house of Israel?

26 But ye have borne the tabernacle of your Moloch and Chiun your images, the star of your god, which ye made to yourselves.

27 Therefore will I cause you to go into captivity beyond Damascus, saith the LORD, whose name is The God of hosts.

A quick read of this text might make one wonder if Amos is asking a real question. But a closer study confirms that it is indeed rhetorical. Further solidifying Amos as one of the most sarcastic, and hence my favorite writer of the minor prophets.

First off we know Israel's history, they were a continually rebellious people.

Deuteronomy 9:24
Ye have been rebellious against the LORD from the day that I knew you.

It is also interesting that Stephen quotes Amos 5:25-26 in Act chapter 7 just before they rock him to sleep.

Acts 7:42
Then God turned, and gave them up to worship the host of heaven; as it is written in the book of the prophets, O ye house of Israel, have ye offered to me slain beasts and sacrifices by the space of forty years in the wilderness?
43 Yea, ye took up the tabernacle of Moloch, and the star of your god Remphan, figures which ye made to worship them: and I will carry you away beyond Babylon.

It is interesting that Stephen uses the word Remphan for the word Chiun. This seems to be a reference to their desire to worship the stars, or the constellations. This is made even more clear by the other statement Amos makes in the passage. *"The star of your god."*

So Amos is asking them sarcastically in verse 25, *"have you always worshipped God and God alone?"* Then he answers that question in the next verse. No, you worshiped the god of the Ammonites and the other false gods of the nations around you!

This is why Amos reminds them so many times throughout his preaching, and why he ends this chapter with the fourth reminder of who God is. *"Saith the LORD* (Jehovah), *The God of hosts."*

PERSONAL NOTES

CHAPTER 6

When God says Woe, He means Woe!

Amos 6:1

Woe to them that are at ease in Zion, and trust in the mountain of Samaria, which are named chief of the nations, to whom the house of Israel came!

The word *"Woe"* is an interesting word. It's not like we use in the English language today. Anytime you see the word woe in the Bible, it is an expression of great lamentation, sorrow, or warning.

This woe, this warning, is not just to a particular people but a people with a particular attitude or mindset, *"them that are at ease,"* and also a misplaced trust or sense of security, *"trust in the mountain of Samaria."*

In other words Amos is telling them this. They have placed their trust, their security in the governing body of Israel, *"mountain of Samaria."* They have grown lax in their service to God, *"them that are at ease."* They have gotten lazy in their service for God. And God is telling them that they are on dangerous grounds by doing this.

You see they've grown into a rhythm. They have grown cold and indifferent to God. God in his mercy doesn't send judgment immediately, and because of this we get the attitude that God isn't going to judge us for our sins.

Ecclesiastes 8:11

Because sentence against an evil work is not executed speedily, therefore the heart of the sons of men is fully set in them to do evil.

So the more God gives grace and mercy the colder they grow, thinking God will not bring judgment. Until they finally arrive at the place that they are in now. God has sent His man to warn of His wrath, and no one is listening.

Again I have to remind myself, Amos is not speaking to America here, but to Israel. Sad that there are so many similarities between the two. America of our day, Israel of Amos' day. It is truly scary.

God has blessed America, God has been patient with America. And just like the people in Amos' day, we are mixing pagan worship with the worship of God, and calling it Biblical worship. But just as in Amos' day, when God was not pleased with what they called worship, you can rest assured that God is not pleased with much of what is taking place in America today in the name of Christianity. There is a judgment coming.

Amos 6:2

Pass ye unto Calneh, and see; and from thence go ye to Hamath the great: then go down to Gath of the Philistines: be they better than these kingdoms? or their border greater than your border?

Calneh was an ancient city built by Nimrod.

Genesis 10:10

And the beginning of his kingdom was Babel, and Erech, and Accad, and Calneh, in the land of Shinar.

Hamath was once a great city of Syria. It is mentioned 32 times in Scripture. It was taken by Assyria and assimilated into the Assyrian kingdom

Then he mentions a third city in this verse. Gath. Gath was a chief city of the Philistines, as we've already mentioned in chapter 1 when we talked about the different cities mentioned in God's judgment on the Philistines. Gath has already been destroyed. That was done by King Uzziah in II Chronicles 26.

Amos brings up these three cities because at one time they were looked at as impenetrable titans of their day. There was a time when no army could come against them. But now, by the time that Amos is prophesying, all three of these cities lie in ruin.

Amos is telling Israel in verse 2, *"don't think that what happened to them cannot happen to you."* We have seen that all through history. Cities or nations reach their pinnacle and seem completely untouchable only to fall later in dramatic fashion.

Not only these previously mentioned cities, but history tells us that Samaria did fall as did Assyria, Babylon, Rome, and Jerusalem. There is no such thing as a city or a nation that is too big to fail no matter what the American congress may say, (bank bailouts). If America continues on the path we are going, we will fall one day as well.

Israel's thought process back then was the same as America's today. *"We have God on our side."* But the fact that Israel was God's chosen people did not give them a free pass to sin. The same way that America's godly and biblical heritage does not afford us the ability to live free of consequence of the sins that plague our land. God will judge America the same as he judged Israel. Paul explains this beautifully in Romans.

Romans 11:20

Well; because of unbelief they were broken off, and thou standest by faith. Be not highminded, but fear:

21 For if God spared not the natural branches, take heed lest he also spare not thee.

Amos continues on.

Amos 6:3

Ye that put far away the evil day, and cause the seat of violence to come near;

4 That lie upon beds of ivory, and stretch themselves upon their couches, and eat the lambs out of the flock, and the calves out of the midst of the stall;

5 That chant to the sound of the viol, and invent to themselves instruments of musick, like David;

6 That drink wine in bowls, and anoint themselves with the chief ointments: but they are not grieved for the affliction of Joseph.

Have you ever heard someone begin to address a certain group of people, and they are so vague at the beginning of their speech that you are not sure exactly who they are talking about? However they get more and more specific as they go until there is no doubt who they are talking about, and the specifics of the what, when and where?

This is what Amos had done here. In verse 1 he starts out, *"Woe to them that are at ease in Zion."* Thats a pretty broad brush. There could have been some that were right with God but were still at ease.

So Amos breaks it down even further, *"and trust in the mountain of Samaria."* We've already discussed in the first few paragraphs of this chapter what he is talking about with this statement. They are trusting in their governmental officials rather than God!

It's almost like Amos starts addressing a certain group of people in verse 1, pauses, and then gives them the warning of verse two. The warning to look at those other cities that thought they were God's gift to the world and see what happened to them. Then in verse three, he continues to narrow down exactly who he is addressing.

Amos 6:3

Ye that put far away the evil day, and cause the seat of violence to come near;

With that first statement of verse 3, we see there were those that completely disregarded the judgment of God. They dismissed it as if God would overlook their sin, or perhaps He could not be bothered with such small things as their affairs. Whatever their reasoning, they saw the judgment of God as something that was so foreign to them that they had no worries.

But Amos tells them that it is not only closer than they think, but their dismissive attitude toward God is ushering it in even faster, *"and cause the seat of violence to come near."*

Amos 6:4

That lie upon beds of ivory, and stretch themselves upon their couches, and eat the lambs out of the flock, and the calves out of the midst of the stall;

Now someone might take verse 4 and say that we ought to have nothing nice because God is condemning them for their beds of ivory. Their sin is not in having soft fluffy couches or beautiful beds of ivory. Their sin was that these things were the center and reason of their entire existence!

It's not a sin to have nice things. But when those nice things become your priority in life and you are willing to sacrifice your relationship with God, your correct worship to God, and trample over your fellow man to get those things, that is when it becomes sin. The sin was not that they had the things. The sin was that the things had them.

This reference to the *"lambs out of the flock,"* and *"the calves out of the midst of the stall"* is again a reference to their extravagant lifestyle. In other words Amos is saying this. They have those among them that are starving to death because of the unsavory business practices of the wealthy, yet the wealthy are eating meals from Michelin star restaurants. They are oppressing the hungry widows while casually eating Wagyu beef for brunch.

All while rejecting God, practicing false worship, and engaging in idolatrous worship. And God has had enough.

Amos 6:5

That chant to the sound of the viol, and invent to themselves instruments of musick, like David;

Worship is largely tied to music today. But just because we sing a spiritual song, does not mean that we are worshipping God. Worship is an attitude of the heart, and if our hearts are in tune with God, then worship will involve much more of our lives than just singing.

However, this is not what they are doing here. Notice the wording of the verse. They are not singing to God, they are not singing for God, they are singing for themselves, *"and invent to themselves instruments of musick."*

Music was intended to be exclusively used in the worship of God. The words “sang”, “song,” and “sing,” all appear for the first time in the Bible in the very same verse, Exodus 15:1. It was in praise to God for His deliverance of the children of Israel from Egypt.

Songs and music can be used for sadness and mourning. This world certainly uses it in that fashion, but that was not the use that God purposed it for. Remember in Psalms 137 what the children of Israel said when they entered Babylonian captivity?

Psalms 137:2

We hanged our harps upon the willows in the midst thereof.

3 For there they that carried us away captive required of us a song; and they that wasted us required of us mirth, saying, Sing us one of the songs of Zion.

4 How shall we sing the LORD's song in a strange land?

Music and songs are supposed to lift up the name of the Lord, they are supposed to encourage us not bring us down to depression or despair.

Paul and Silas started singing at midnight in Acts 16. They weren't singing *"oh despair and agony."* They weren't singing the blues. They were singing praises in the midst of their troubles!

When trials come, when tribulations surround us, we are not to drown our spirit in songs that drag us down, but we are to sing to encourage ourselves in the Lord.

Jonah 2:9

But I will sacrifice unto thee with the voice of thanksgiving;

I will pay that that I have vowed. Salvation is of the LORD.

Amos continues on;

Amos 6:6

That drink wine in bowls, and anoint themselves with the chief ointments: but they are not grieved for the affliction of Joseph.

This again is speaking to their excess of living. If you live in the southeast of the United States you know that *"Coke"* is universally used to describe any carbonated soft drink. In much the same way *"wine"* is used to describe any fruit of the vine in the Bible regardless of it's fermentation status.

This may well have been speaking of fermented wine, we do not know, but what we do know is that he is condemning their absolute failure to exercise self control in their lives while being completely unphased with their dishonest gain and by their absolute disregard for those that were starving around them.

"They anoint themselves with the chief ointments." And you thought this essential oil movement was a modern 21st century movement! This idea has been around for many, many years. There truly is *"nothing new under the sun."*

Amos 6:7

Therefore now shall they go captive with the first that go captive, and the banquet of them that stretched themselves shall be removed.

Amos makes a chilling declaration as he promises that when the destruction comes and the nation falls, these will be the very first ones to go.

Their cushy life that they once enjoyed will be gone. Their beds of ivory will be demolished. Their soft couches will be burned. Their life of luxury that they once enjoyed will be no more.

What a warning this is to you and me to never let the blessings of God become the priority in our lives. How many times have you seen this happen in someone's life. They don't have a penny to their name, barely making a living, but they love God, they live for God. In turn God blesses them, but then they start focusing on the blessings rather than the blesser. Their priorities get focused on getting more rather than the One who gave them more. Then God has to bring correction into their lives.

Amos 6:8

The Lord GOD hath sworn by himself, saith the LORD the God of hosts, I abhor the excellency of Jacob, and hate his palaces: therefore will I deliver up the city with all that is therein.

Hebrews 6 talks about how when God could swear by no greater, He swear By himself. God is promising on His reputation, on His name. When God promises something, you can rest assured He will not forget, or neglect to do it!

God uses many words in the Bible to describe something that He absolutely hates. Here he uses a word that is only found 18 times in the Bible, abhor. But it is interesting what he abhors in verse 8. He abhors excellency. Excellency in this passage is describing the pride, the haughtiness of Israel.

The fastest way to get on dangerous ground with God, is to get prideful in our hearts and attitudes.

Not only the excellency (pride) but also their palaces. There again, does that mean that every one that had a palace was hated by God just for the simple fact that they had a palace? No, it was not the physical palace that God hated, but it was what that palace had come to represent. It was the sins that they were committing in those palaces that God hated. These palaces were filled with wealth that they had unethically extracted from the poor. *(Chapter 3:10)*

The word palace, or palaces is used 13 times in the book of Amos (interesting number). With the judgment that Amos delivers in the first 2 chapters, from Damascus, Gaza, Tyrus, Edom, Ammon, Moab, Judah, and Israel, he announces judgment on their palaces. In other words judgment is coming from the top down. No one will be spared. Social status, political power, service in the priesthood will not spare the wicked in the day of judgment.

I'm glad that the Bible says that;

2 Peter 2:9

The Lord knoweth how to deliver the godly out of temptations, and to reserve the unjust unto the day of judgment to be punished:

But as for the others, the ungodly. Amos' warning is clear, you will not escape.

Amos 6:9

And it shall come to pass, if there remain ten men in one house, that they shall die.

Amos said that the wicked will not escape the judgment of God. The majority will die, and those that do not will go into captivity.

Amos 6:10

And a man's uncle shall take him up, and he that burneth him, to bring out the bones out of the house, and shall say unto him that is by the sides of the house, Is there yet any with thee? and he shall say, No. Then shall he say, Hold thy tongue: for we may not make mention of the name of the LORD.

Burial has always been God's accepted way of disposing of dead bodies.

Genesis 3:19

In the sweat of thy face shalt thou eat bread, till thou return unto the ground; for out of it wast thou taken: for dust thou art, <u>and unto dust shalt thou return</u>.

Cremation has always been the way of disposal of the bodies of the wicked.

Leviticus 20:14

And if a man take a wife and her mother, it is wickedness: they shall be burnt with fire, both he and they; that there be no wickedness among you.

Leviticus 21:9

And the daughter of any priest, if she profane herself by playing the whore, she profaneth her father: she shall be burnt with fire.

We see further examples of this in the disposing of the body of Saul.

I Samuel 31:12

All the valiant men arose, and went all night, and took the body of Saul and the bodies of his sons from the wall of Bethshan, and came to Jabesh, and burnt them there.

Can you imagine the horrendous scene, being part of the ones that had to stay behind and burn the bodies of the dead that did not want to submit to God?

Verse 10 of Amos chapter 6 makes me think of another similar scene in the Bible. In Leviticus chapter 10 the sons of Aaron, Nadab and Abihu, offered strange fire to the Lord. They did this in direct disobedience to God. God immediately sent fire down and the Bible says that it, *"devoured them, and they died before the LORD."* It is interesting that the Bible says that Moses calls for the sons of Uzziel, the UNCLE of Aaron to carry out the bodies. Moses gives them strict instructions in this chapter to hold their peace just as Amos gives them in our verse at hand, *"hold thy tongue."*

So what is the significance of that statement, what is the take away? I believe it is this. When God's judgment falls after repeated warnings, and after He has clearly laid out His instructions yet they continually choose to ignore or discount them, they'd better not say a word. *"God is unfair, God is so cruel."* No, God gave warning after warning, and they refused to heed the warning, now the consequences are inevitable.

Amos 6:11

For, behold, the LORD commandeth, and he will smite the great house with breaches, and the little house with clefts.

Again, Amos gives a confirmation about God's faithfulness to do what He said He would do. This wonderful city, this fortress that is built to attest to your ability and great work, the solid wall will one day be left in rubble!

Amos 6:12

Shall horses run upon the rock? will one plow there with oxen? for ye have turned judgment into gall, and the fruit of righteousness into hemlock:

I was born in Louisiana. Catholicism is ramped in our state. When I was growing up and someone asked a question in which the answer was a resounding yes, ie, *"do you want a piece of cake?"* A common response you might hear would be, *"is the Pope catholic?"* So what does this little example have to do with anything you may ask?

Amos is using two ridiculous situations to prove his point. Just as obvious as it is that they would not run their horses through the rocks because it would likely break a leg, or plow in that same area because it would not yield any fruit. It is obvious that God will bring judgment on the nation of Israel.

For the most part we think of God bringing judgment for the purpose of bringing destruction. Although that is sometimes the case, it doesn't have to be. God's purpose and plan for bringing judgment is to bring us to repentance and ultimately restoration of fellowship.

But for Israel, because of their determination to rebel and refusal to get right, when Amos tells them, *"for ye have turned judgment into gall"* he is telling them that the judgment God brought into their lives was with the intention to turn them back to him. Had they obeyed it would have ended in restoration of fellowship. But because they rebelled it will end in bitterness, gall. The book of Proverbs illustrates this perfectly.

Proverbs 29:1

He, that being often reproved hardeneth his neck, shall suddenly be destroyed, and that without remedy.

He confirms their refusal to get right with the last statement of that verse, *"the fruit of righteousness into hemlock."* Hemlock is bitterness. They have corrupted the good things of God into something bitter and distasteful. So, is God going to bring judgment to the land of Israel? Is the Pope Catholic?

Amos 6:13

Ye which rejoice in a thing of nought, which say, Have we not taken to us horns by our own strength?

They have no desire for God, no pleasure in holy things. They don't rejoice in spiritual things. They rejoice in things that do not matter, *"a thing of nought."* They yawn through church on Sunday morning, then scream their heads off over the football game Sunday afternoon. They don't even spend 5 minutes a week reading their Bible, but spend hours a day on social media. They brag about being a self made man, *"have we not taken to us horns by our own strength?"* How foolish of us to think that we have obtained through our own strength, the things that God has blessed us with! Years later Paul addresses this same attitude with the people of Corinth.

1 Corinthians 4:7

For who maketh thee to differ from another? and what hast thou that thou didst not receive? now if thou didst receive it, why dost thou glory, as if thou hadst not received it?

Sadly this attitude permeates our American culture today. We give *"lip service"* to God by singing God bless America, but then take credit for everything that we have in our lives!

Amos 6:14

But, behold, I will raise up against you a nation, O house of Israel, saith the LORD the God of hosts; and they shall afflict you from the entering in of Hemath unto the river of the wilderness.

Amos is revealing God's judgment progressively. He starts out with a declaration of judgment in Amos 2:2, *"I will punish you."* Vague and general, yet still chilling. In chapter 2:11, he goes a little further into detail when He tells them that it will be *"an adversary."* In chapter 2:14 and 3:2 He gives them insight not so much into the who, but the how, *"visit the transgressions,"* and, *"take you away with hooks."*

But here he goes a little further into the detail of the *"who."* He said, *"I will raise up against you a nation."* Although Amos never names the Assyrians in the book, they were certainly a rising power and a known fierce and violent people.

Regardless if they suspected it to be Assyria or not, God had spoken it. And when God has spoken we can rest assured that He will bring it to pass regardless if we understand the details of it or not!

PERSONAL NOTES

CHAPTER 7

The Finality of Judgment

Amos 7:1

Thus hath the Lord GOD shewed unto me; and, behold, he formed grasshoppers in the beginning of the shooting up of the latter growth; and, lo, it was the latter growth after the king's mowings.

2 And it came to pass, that when they had made an end of eating the grass of the land, then I said, O Lord GOD, forgive, I beseech thee: by whom shall Jacob arise? for he is small.

3 The LORD repented for this: It shall not be, saith the LORD.

When I first started studying the book of Amos years ago, chapter 7 is the chapter that really made an impression on me. It is heartbreaking because we see everything coming to a head.

We have seen the pattern over and over throughout the book. God's mercy and patience exhibited. Israel's refusal to heed the warning and to get right. But now in chapter 7 there is a change in the tone of Amos.

Chapter 7 is quite different from the preceding 6 chapter's of Amos. We see God drawing a line on Israel and saying, *"I'm done."*

The first eight words are key to this chapter, *"Thus hath the Lord God shewed unto me."* This will be a common thought as we go through these next two chapters.

In chapter 1 verse 1, Amos is speaking of himself when he says, *"which he saw concerning Israel."* He takes a chapter and a half to tell of God's judgment on surrounding nations. He then spends the next 4 and a half chapters describing the sin, rebellion, and stubbornness of Israel. Oh, there have been mentions of God's judgment in these verses, but that was not the emphasis. The emphasis was Israel's sins and what has led them to this point.

So in those first 6 chapters Amos is primarily describing what God showed him about Israel's sins. Starting in chapter 7, Amos is primarily describing what God has showed him about Israel's punishment. Not just that, but the finality of God's punishment.

Amos describes 2 different instances in these first 3 verses. As a judgment for Israel's rebellion, God prepared grasshoppers (locust) to devour their field. A swarm of locust can be absolutely devastating to a landscape. They can quite literally strip an area completely bare of any vegetation within a day, then move on to the next location.

In those days the loving and benevolent king (imagine an eye roll emoji here) would take the first harvest of hay for himself. That was their *"taxes"* that the people had to pay.

But God said that after the first cutting of the king's hay, and the grass began to come back up, when the fields began to look like there was going to be a second bountiful growth for the people to keep for themselves, that God sent the locust in and devoured all the vegetation. There are some that think this to be metaphorical, but Amos is clear that this is an actual event that took place in Israel.

After seeing this happen, Amos intercedes on the behalf of Israel. He prays for God to spare Israel because they're not as big and strong and independent as they think they are.

Let me pause right here and say that again we see the care that Amos holds for Israel. Some may call Amos cold and callous for the bluntness in which he calls Israel out for their sins. But Amos is only doing this because he loves them, and does not want to see God's judgment fall on this land and on this people.

We live in a culture that sees any form of correction or rebuke as hate. As of the writing of this paragraph we are 6 days removed from the assassination of Charlie Kirk. Warning people of a hurtful and destructive and sinful lifestyle is not hate, quite the contrary, it is the strongest form of love you can show. To affirm sin and wickedness knowing that there are severe consequences for that way of life is the most hateful and careless attitude a person can exhibit.

We can surmise from this text that this was only the beginning of God's wrath that He was planning on pouring out on Israel, Why? Because we see Amos interceding on behalf of the nation, and God changes His mind. Verse 3 *"the LORD repented for this: It shall not be."*

Amos 7:4

Thus hath the Lord GOD shewed unto me: and, behold, the Lord GOD called to contend by fire, and it devoured the great deep, and did eat up a part.

5 Then said I, O Lord GOD, cease, I beseech thee: by whom shall Jacob arise? for he is small.

6 The LORD repented for this: This also shall not be, saith the Lord GOD.

In verses 4 thru 6 we see the same scenario play out. God brings a literal fire in Israel for their sins. God shows Amos that this fire is not random, it didn't just happen. This fire started for one reason, and for one reason only, that is the sins of Israel.

Again Amos falls to his knees and cries out to God, *"I beseech thee!"* That word beseech is a very strong word. Amos is literally begging God, *"Please have mercy and spare Israel!"* This is a great lesson to me and you. We would see a lot more prayers answered today if we had some earnest passion, emotion, and intensity in our prayer life.

Israel had the same problem that you and I have today. A pride problem. They thought that they were something, but what they did not realize is that they were nothing without God, *"by whom shall Jacob arise? For he is small."*

You know how to have real strength in this life? Realize your weakness. Paul put it this way.

2 Corinthians 12:10

Therefore I take pleasure in infirmities, in reproaches, in necessities, in persecutions, in distresses for Christ's sake: for when I am weak, then am I strong.

Oh, if we could only realize how weak and needful we are, what strength we could have in the Lord!

Amos 7:7

Thus he shewed me: and, behold, the Lord stood upon a wall made by a plumbline, with a plumbline in his hand.

8 And the LORD said unto me, Amos, what seest thou? And I said, A plumbline. Then said the Lord, Behold, I will set a plumbline in the midst of my people Israel: I will not again pass by them any more:

This is the third different scenario that God shows Amos in just the first few verses of chapter 7. But we see a change in the way that this one happens.

If you are a builder, or have any background in construction as I do, you'll understand clearly what Amos is talking about here. But if you do not have that background, let me lay it out for you.

I always chuckle at those that say we should not use illustrations in our preaching. Now granted, our preaching should not be all illustrations and no Bible, but illustrations are useful in proving a finer point. And God uses an illustration here with Amos.

In this illustration the Lord is standing upon a wall, with a plumbline in His hand. We use levels to check if an object is square. If we did not have levels our houses would truly look like our drawings from when we were a kid.

But a plumb line is used to check "true vertical." If you are unfamiliar with what a plumb line is, it is simply a piece of string that has a weight attached to the bottom of it. That weight will come to a point. And it is used to check if the wall, or object being built is as vertical as possible. Nothing better in testing this than gravity.

So when Amos uses this illustration of a plumb line he is saying that God is testing Israel for *"true vertical."* He wanted them to see how they measure up and the results are not good!

What is interesting here is that God did not delegate out this responsibility to an angel or a prophet, it is God Himself that is judging Israel. This is biblically consistent. God may use an angel or a prophet to deliver messages in the Bible, but when it comes time to judging people for their sin, God reserves this task for Himself.

No doubt many accused Amos of being judgmental. They probably used the same saying that many cry out today, *"only God can judge me."* Amos was not trying to judge them, Amos was trying to warn them. They refused to heed the warning of Amos and now they are getting exactly what they asked for. They are being judged by God Almighty!

The scariest statement of the entire book of Amos occurs right here in chapter 7 verse 8 when God tells Amos, *"I will not again pass by them any more."*

Amos has watched twice as God has brought judgment to Israel through the locust and through the fire. Amos falls to his knees both times and cries out to God on behalf of a nation that laughs in the face of Amos, and in the face of God. Both times God had mercy on an ungrateful nation because of one broken hearted prophet. But here in verse 8 God is telling Amos of another judgment that is coming. It is almost like God pauses and tells Amos, *"I know that you've interceded on Israel's behalf twice, so I'm going to tell you before you even ask, Don't! Don't bother with interceding on their behalf, because I will not change my mind this time."*

What a terrifying thought that you and I can push God to His limit where He draws a line and tells others not to pray for us. But that is exactly what has happened here. And this is not the only time that God commanded a prophet not to pray for someone.

Hosea 4:17
Ephraim is joined to idols: <u>let him alone</u>.

Jeremiah 7:16

Therefore pray not thou for this people, neither lift up cry nor prayer for them, neither make intercession to me: <u>for I will not hear thee</u>.

What a solemn reminder for us to keep short accounts with God. Not to live in rebellion but to walk in fellowship with Him.

Amos 7:9

And the high places of Isaac shall be desolate, and the sanctuaries of Israel shall be laid waste; and I will rise against the house of Jeroboam with the sword.

God in verse 9 announces judgment against the false religion of Israel, *"the high places"* and *"the sanctuaries."* Way back when the first Jeroboam set up the golden calfs and the false worship, God said it will be laid waste.

Also in this verse God announces judgment against the corrupt political system of the day. God did not say that judgment would come against Jeroboam, but against the house of Jeroboam. In fact Jeroboam was no longer ruler over Israel when they fell to Assyria. We see once again that the Word of God is accurate in every detail!

A Personal Attack

Amos 7:10

Then Amaziah the priest of Bethel sent to Jeroboam king of Israel, saying, Amos hath conspired against thee in the midst of the house of Israel: the land is not able to bear all his words.

11 For thus Amos saith, Jeroboam shall die by the sword, and Israel shall surely be led away captive out of their own land.

Now it is no surprise that the sniveling little weasel of a priest didn't like Amos' preaching. Just in case you think that I'm being too hard on the priest, Amaziah, let me remind you that he is not a man of integrity. Remember how the Bible tells us in II Kings 12 when Jeroboam came to rule over Israel that he, *"made priests of the lowest of the people."* That has been 150 years or more in the past that Jeroboam did that, but keep in mind that Israel has never had a godly king. In this 150 years Israel has gotten worse in their rebellion against God not better. So I believe it would be safe in saying that they are still choosing priests of the lowest of the people.

And if that is not enough proof that Amaziah has as much business being in the priestly position as a billy goat, look at how he exercises his power in verse 11.

From the middle of verse 10, through verse 11 Amaziah is talking to the king about Amos. He does nothing but lie about Amos.

"Amos hath conspired against thee." Amos has not conspired against the king at all. There is no plot to dismantle the kingdom or to assassinate the king. Amos is announcing God's judgment against Israel.

"For thus Amos saith, Jeroboam shall die by the sword." Again, this is nothing more than a twisting of Amos' words. Liberal tactics (political or religious) do not change. They always look to twist words and make you say something that you did not intend to say. Let me remind you of something that we stated just a few paragraphs ago. Amos never said that the sword would come against Jeroboam but against his house. But this is all that Amaziah needed to go running to the king with false accusations against the prophet of God.

Amos 7:12

Also Amaziah said unto Amos, O thou seer, go, flee thee away into the land of Judah, and there eat bread, and prophesy there:

13 But prophesy not again any more at Bethel: for it is the king's chapel, and it is the king's court.

After Amaziah has run to the king to tattle on Amos, like a 6 years old throwing a tantrum. In verses 12 and 13 he proceeds to launch a barrage of personal attacks at Amos.

"O thou seer," in the Bible days a prophet was also called a seer. However I do not believe that Amaziah is showing respect to Amos when he referred to him as a seer. I would imagine that this is a mocking tone that Amaziah is taking with Amos.

"Go back home, we don't like your kind around here." This is what Amaziah is telling Amos, *"go, flee thee away into the land of Judah."* Judah was where Amos was from.

He was accusing Amos of being in the ministry for the money, *"there eat bread."* How sad that the world thinks of the ministry as a lucrative career. If you are a pastor, missionary, or evangelist I will pause here to give you a chance to stop laughing. I don't know about you but I have, and still could again, make much more money working in this world than in the ministry. But this is not a career, it is a calling.

Amos 7:13

But prophesy not again any more at Bethel: for it is the king's chapel, and it is the king's court.

Stop and consider what Amaziah is saying here. Jerusalem is where they were to conduct worship, to carry out the sacrifices, to observe the feasts of Leviticus 23, but over the course of the last 150 or so years they have drifted so far away from the truth that the emphasis is put on Bethel over Jerusalem. This confusion carries over to the Samaritans in the New Testament.

John 4:20

Our fathers worshipped in this mountain; and ye say, that in Jerusalem is the place where men ought to worship.

Also notice that the authority Amaziah ascribes to the king is greater that what he gives to the priest, or to God! *"This is the king's chapel, it is the king's court, and God has no jurisdiction here,"* is in essence what Amaziah is saying. When we begin to observe the laws of man over the laws of God, when we begin to put the authority of the government over the authority of God, we are on dangerous ground.

A Personal Judgment

Amos 7:14

Then answered Amos, and said to Amaziah, I was no prophet, neither was I a prophet's son; but I was an herdman, and a gatherer of sycomore fruit:

15 And the LORD took me as I followed the flock, and the LORD said unto me, Go, prophesy unto my people Israel.

This is probably the second most well known verse from the book of Amos. It is a verse used many times in jest, but an important and sobering verse none the less. Amos is very clear to state that his authority did not come from man. His ministry was not ordained by the local seminary, but was ordained by God himself. Amos was what we could call just a blue collar worker. A *"good ole boy"* if he lived in the southeastern United States. But he was a man with a calling and a burden on his heart to preach the message that God had given him.

Amos did not follow the typical pattern of the young men of that day. He was not one of the *"sons of the prophets."* To put it in our language, he did not go to Bible college as I mentioned at the beginning of this book. I'm afraid that too many young men today look at the ministry as a *"career choice."* They go to a Bible college, get their degree in divinity or doctrinal studies. Then they want to go out and *"get on staff"* at a large church (sounds like an infection to me.) They want a full time salary because Heaven forbid they have to work a secular job!

The ministry is not a career choice, it is a calling. Sometimes we have to work and get our hands dirty to provide for our families. If the Lord provides and allows a ministry to be full time that is a tremendous blessing, but that should not be the deciding factor for a young man when considering a position at a church, it honestly should not be a factor at all. The only thing that should factor into the equation is, *"does God want me here?"* I personally think that the worst thing that could happen to a young preacher is to get on full time staff at a church somewhere. Work builds character, and that is something that young preachers are in short supply of these days.

Amos 7:16

Now therefore hear thou the word of the LORD: Thou sayest, Prophesy not against Israel, and drop not thy word against the house of Isaac.

Here in verse 16 Amos is about to deliver a chilling prophecy against Amaziah personally. This is the only personal judgment delivered in the book of Amos. The entirety of the book of Amos, with the exception of the end of chapter 7, is God's judgment against a rebellious nation. Here at the end of chapter 7 we have God's judgment against a rebellious priest. But before Amos does this he wants to make sure that Amaziah and everyone else knows the reason why.

It's not because Amaziah has falsely accused Amos, lied about him, or questioned Amos' motives. It is because he has misused and misrepresented his responsibilities as a priest.

Amaziah should have been the one delivering God's message to the people. Amaziah should have been the one standing for righteousness and the law of God. Instead, he was too concerned about pleasing the king, about lining his own pockets by buddying up to the upper class of Israel instead of calling out their sin. Had Amaziah done his job, God would have had no need to call Amos from his little farm in Tekoa to preach to Israel.

Amos 7:17

Therefore thus saith the LORD; Thy wife shall be an harlot in the city, and thy sons and thy daughters shall fall by the sword, and thy land shall be divided by line; and thou shalt die in a polluted land: and Israel shall surely go into captivity forth of his land.

By compromising, Amaziah thought he was providing for his family. He thought he was doing what he could to provide the best life possible for his wife and children.

Like many men today, Amaziah sacrificed the spiritual provisions of his family for the physical provisions. Like many men today, he put more emphasis on making a living and what he could obtain in this life without the consideration of what it would cost him in the long run. And like many men, he finds out too late that the cost of these decisions are far worse than what he had gained by forsaking the commandments of God.

Amos said that the wife of Amaziah would become a prostitute on the streets. His precious land that he worked so hard to maintain would be divided and given to others. His children would be killed by the sword probably dying in the 90% that die in the battles with Assyria before the fall. But Amaziah would live, only to be carried off to Assyria to die in a foreign land.

All through the Bible up till present day the old saying still rings true "*Sin will take you farther than you wanted to go, leave you longer than you wanted to stay, and cost you more than you wanted to pay.*"

PERSONAL NOTES

CHAPTER 8

Ripe for Harvest

Amos 8:1

Thus hath the Lord GOD shewed unto me: and behold a basket of summer fruit.

2 And he said, Amos, what seest thou? And I said, A basket of summer fruit. Then said the LORD unto me, The end is come upon my people of Israel; I will not again pass by them any more.

In Chapter 7 Amos shows us God's judgment in the parable of the grasshoppers, the fire, and the plumb line. Then it is almost like he is interrupted in the middle of his preaching with the exchange between he and Amaziah the priest.

Amaziah tells Amos what he thinks of him, and in turn Amos tells Amaziah what God thinks about him. Now, I'm not a debater, but I'm pretty sure that Amos won that exchange. That really brings into focus the following verse.

Romans 8:31

What shall we then say to these things? If God be for us, who can be against us?

Then we get into chapter 8, and it's as if Amos picks right back up where he left off in chapter 7:9. In the same context of Amos announcing God's judgment in the example of the plumb line, he uses the illustration of a basket of summer fruit.

Harvest time is generally seen as a happy time. A time to reap the fruits of your labor that you have invested your blood, sweat, and tears into all summer long. But if you have been sowing seeds of sin, rebellion, and unrighteousness, as Israel has been doing, then harvest time is not a time of joy, but a time of weeping and mourning.

The bill always comes due, and for Israel the time is coming that they pay for their sin. When God showed Amos a basket of summer fruit, He is showing him that Israel is ripe for harvest. What a dreadful and frightening thought. No wonder the Bible said the following.

Hebrews 10:31

It is a fearful thing to fall into the hands of the living God.

It is also interesting that God finished this illustration of the basket of summer fruit the same way he finishes up the plumb line illustration. *"I will not again pass by them anymore."*

Again God tells Amos not to intercede on behalf of Israel, because he will not have mercy again, not without repentance on the part of Israel. In the first two judgments, the locust and the fire, God repented (changed His mind) without repentance on Israel's part, without them falling on their face and begging for forgiveness. God granted mercy solely on the interceding of Amos. But now, the only thing that can save Israel is not Amos begging for forgiveness on behalf of Israel, but for Israel to beg for their own forgiveness.

Thank God we can pray, and intercede on behalf of someone else. But just as God will not save someone who does not want to be saved no matter how fervently we pray for them to, God will not continue to forgive someone solely off the prayers of someone else. There comes a time when that person that is living in sin will have to repent in order for God not to bring judgment into their life.

Amos 8:3

And the songs of the temple shall be howlings in that day, saith the Lord GOD: there shall be many dead bodies in every place; they shall cast them forth with silence.

At first read, this sounds like a tame verse compared to the rest of the book of Amos. But it is in fact quite chilling.

This temple that on occasion rang with laughter and joyous singing of the deliverance and glory of God. At other times it sounded with singing that was remorseful over sin. But now there is no longer songs of joy, no longer songs of repentance. As a matter of fact the sounds coming out of the temple are not songs at all, but they are howlings and crying because of the judgment that God has brought into the land because of their sins.

The last half of this verse makes me think of the holocaust. I've read the stories that describe the horrors of what the soldiers saw and smelled when they first walked on the scene of the Bergen Belsen concentration camp. Can you imagine walking up to the gates of the compound on that day in 1945, the stench of rotting corpses in the air. Ten thousand dead bodies in different stages of decomposition littering the ground. Those that were still alive just walking around in a zombie-like state, their minds reduced to jello over what they have seen and experienced and lived through in those camps. After the camp is secured, they soon had to start working on the process of disposing of the bodies that were lying on the ground. How could you perform that task in anything other than stunned silence over the atrocities that you are witnessing.

This is the scene that Amos is describing to Israel here. The 3 year besiegement by Assyria of Samaria has left 90% of the people of Israel dead. The rest are lead away captive. But just as in WW2 when they made the captured SS soldiers work to dispose of the corpses, disposing of the bodies of the Israelites is not a task that the Assyrians cared to do.

So the obvious thing to do would be to make the captured Jews dispose of the bodies of their friends and families. How else would you be able to perform this task other than utter stunned silence? *"They shall cast them forth with silence."*

A Desire for Wealth

Amos 8:4

Hear this, O ye that swallow up the needy, even to make the poor of the land to fail,

5 Saying, When will the new moon be gone, that we may sell corn? and the sabbath, that we may set forth wheat, making the ephah small, and the shekel great, and falsifying the balances by deceit?

6 That we may buy the poor for silver, and the needy for a pair of shoes; yea, and sell the refuse of the wheat?

After telling them of the judgments that were stayed because of the prayers of Amos, and how God had decided that His mercy was no longer available without their repentance. After the conversation with Amaziah, the false accusations that he made against Amos, and the chilling personal prophecy that Amos gave Amaziah. Amos gets back to addressing the people that God has sent him to warn.

We already know that they were worshipping in the wrong location. For the last 150 years they were worshipping in Dan and Bethel when Jerusalem is the place that God commanded them to keep the feasts. In verse 5 Amos tells us that their worship was empty and hollow.

On one hand you want to commend them for at least being faithful. However, it is difficult to give them kudos for faithfulness because the practices that they were being faithful to keep were unscriptural. But then you realize that their heart was not even in it. The feelings of their heart are betrayed by the words of their mouths, *"When will the new moon be gone."*

We see that they were keeping the feast, but their heart and their mind were on their business. Much like Christians today. They may come to church, they may even be faithful to every service and every revival meeting, but in their hearts and in their minds they are AWOL. Physically their body is in church, but mentally they are thinking about dinner, or about the ball game, or where they are going to put their deer stand to get the best shot on the 10 point that they got on the trail cam last week.

As if that wasn't bad enough, their business was not even an honest business. It was intentionally dishonest. Their longing was to swindle their neighbors out of as much money as possible, *"making the ephah small, and the shekel great, and falsifying the balances by deceit."*

The ephah was their bushel. It is a measurement of their harvest. So when the small farmer would bring his crop to sell at market, these sly business men would do their best to tip the balances out of the favor of the seller by leaving some of the grain off of the scale, *"making the ephah small,"* and tip the balance into their favor, *"and the shekel great."* It was a "double wammie"of sorts. The shekel is what they would use to counter balance the scale to weigh the wheat. So they would rig their system to make the wheat lighter than it really was and their weight that they used to measure the wheat larger than it was supposed to be.

They made money on the buying of the goods and on the selling of the goods. We see their dishonesty in this as well, *"sell the refuse of the wheat."* So they would take the chaff, bundle it in with some of the good wheat, and sell that for food. The unsuspecting buyer would get it home only to find out that there is a bunch of worthless chaff in the wheat that they bought to feed their family. So now you have a triple whammie. And those that could not pay their bills, were sold into slavery, *"That we may buy the poor for silver, and the needy for a pair of shoes."* Now you have a quadruple wammie. It did not matter the situation or the circumstance, the upper class of Israel were going to come out on top of the financial mountain.

Keep in mind that this was all being practiced by *"good church going people."* This is a prime example of what John wrote about in Revelation chapter 3. *"I would thou wert cold or hot."* They were thinking just because they had a *"form of godliness"* that they were ok. God is not interested in our spiritual play acting. He is interested in how we are living.

Amos 8:7

The LORD hath sworn by the excellency of Jacob, Surely I will never forget any of their works.

In Amos 4:2 the Bible said that, *"the Lord GOD hath sworn by his holiness,"* and Amos 6:8 says, *"The LORD hath sworn by himself."* So this is just another way of saying the same thing. God is the excellency of Jacob, and He has sworn by himself that he will not forget Israel's sins.

This is a terrifying verse. Amos is telling Israel that they will not get away with the sins that they are committing. God has a good memory, and He will not forget or overlook sin! Paul makes this abundantly clear.

Galatians 6:7

Be not deceived; God is not mocked: for whatsoever a man soweth, that shall he also reap.

The old preachers used to say, *"God doesn't always pay on Friday, but He always pays."* Saved or lost, God will not let sin slide. As a child of God we are going to Heaven, and there is nothing that will change that, but Hebrews chapter 12 clearly teaches us that God will chasten His children.

Amos 8:8

Shall not the land tremble for this, and every one mourn that dwelleth therein? and it shall rise up wholly as a flood; and it shall be cast out and drowned, as by the flood of Egypt.

Amos is pointing back to the events that took place in Egypt. Although these events were hundreds of years earlier, it was still taught and talked about how God delivered Israel from Egypt. I do believe, however, that this was a hollow memorial.

Much like the average American today that goes to a sporting event and takes his hat off during the prayer and the singing of God Bless America, but as soon as the song is over he cracks open his beer and cusses God the rest of the day. Just because he gave audible credit to God for His "blessings" on America does not make him a God fearing American.

By this same token, Israel may have been paying "lip service" to God by telling their children about God delivering them from Egypt. But now they are the ones living contrary to God's law and God's commandments.

So as Amos is reminding Israel about the plagues of the land during the Egyptian captivity, and just like the land heaved and trembled for the unjustness of the Egyptians against Israel, this land would now heave and tremble for the oppression and idolatry that is in the land of Israel.

Just as the Israelites cried out to God for deliverance from the oppression of Egypt, the oppressed Israelites have cried out to God, and He is about to deliver the oppressed Israelites out of the hand of the oppressive Israelites.

Amos 8:9

And it shall come to pass in that day, saith the Lord GOD, that I will cause the sun to go down at noon, and I will darken the earth in the clear day:

This verse is interesting and perplexing. There are several different thoughts or ideas that go along with this verse. Some believe that it is talking about an eclipse. This, in my opinion, is the least likely of the scenarios.

Some believe that it is a reference to the end time. That is interesting when you consider the verse in the light of Joel 2:2. When Joel is talking about the day of the Lord he said that it is, *"A day of darkness and of gloominess."* And Matthew 24:29 says, *"Immediately after the tribulation of those days shall the sun be darkened, and the moon shall not give her light."*

It is interesting also that when you compare this to Revelation 6 it seems to line up as well for an end time meaning.

Revelation 6:12

And I beheld when he had opened the sixth seal, and, lo, there was a great earthquake; and the sun became black as sackcloth of hair, and the moon became as blood;

So it seems that verses 8 and 9 of Amos chapter 8, the *"trembling of the land"*, and the *"sun going down at noon"*, lines up perfectly with the opening of the sixth seal of Revelation 6.

Some have said that this *"sun going down at noon"* is a reference to their sudden destruction in the midst of prosperity. That would certainly go along with Biblical teaching.

Proverbs 29:1

He, that being often reproved hardeneth his neck, shall suddenly be destroyed, and that without remedy.

I personally think that this may be a little of both. I think that Amos is telling them that they will face a sudden fall for their sin when it all looks like sunshine, rainbows, and unicorns.

But like so many of the Old Testament prophets, their prophecies have a near and future fulfillment. We know from history that they were indeed cut down in what would seem their prime. But I also believe that Amos is pulling back the curtain a little right here and showing us events that are still future to us as well.

Amos 8:10

And I will turn your feasts into mourning, and all your songs into lamentation; and I will bring up sackcloth upon all loins, and baldness upon every head; and I will make it as the mourning of an only son, and the end thereof as a bitter day.

The book of Amos is a difficult book to preach and to teach from. Not because it is difficult to understand, but because it is very simple to understand. And in that simplicity we see the wrath of a just and Almighty God!

All through the book of Amos so far we have discussed God's wrath. Oh there have been moments of tender mercies that have shown through, but most of the book has been a very direct, straight, hard dose of God's anger against sin.

Here in Amos 8:10, we are nearing the end of the book. And Amos is giving us a summary in this verse of what the book covers. You could almost describe this verse as a *"table of contents"* for the book. He lists 6 things here that God will do to punish Israel. This is a culmination of judgments that He has told of in other places in Scripture.

The first two he covers are, *"I will turn your feasts into mourning,"* and, *"all your songs into lamentation."* This is something that He will remind them of again a few years later with Hosea.

Hosea 2:11

I will also cause all her mirth to cease, her feast days, her new moons, and her sabbaths, and all her solemn feasts.

The next two things Amos tells them is, *"I will bring up sackcloth upon all loins, and baldness upon every head."* This is told to Judah years later when they are under Babylonian captivity.

Ezekiel 7:18

They shall also gird themselves with sackcloth, and horror shall cover them; and shame shall be upon all faces, and baldness upon all their heads.

These terms don't really mean much to us these days, but these were symbols of great mourning and sorrow to Israel. Yet, what amazes me the most is that these warnings went largely unheeded.

The end of verse 10 is the most terrifying part of the verse, and maybe of the entire book this far. A persons greatest fear as a parent is something happening to their children.

To go childless in the sick society that we live in is seen almost as a badge of honor, but to be childless or barren in Old Testament times was the ultimate disgrace. Imagine being a couple in Amos' day, God has only seen fit to allow you to have one child, and now that child has been taken away.

I've heard some compare this to the weeping and mourning described in verse 10 comparable to Egypt when the death angel visited during the first Passover.

Exodus 12:30

And Pharaoh rose up in the night, he, and all his servants, and all the Egyptians; and there was a great

cry in Egypt; for there was not a house where there was not one dead.

I cannot help but imagine that this is a worse situation. This is not just the first born. Losing a child would be excruciating enough. Imagine if it was your only child. God said that this is what their suffering would be like.

A Famine of Hearing

Amos 8:11

Behold, the days come, saith the Lord GOD, that I will send a famine in the land, not a famine of bread, nor a thirst for water, but of hearing the words of the LORD:

I stated that verse 14 of the previous chapter was probably the second most well know verse from the book of Amos. Here we have probably the most well known verse. Used many times to describe the spiritual condition of our day. All though that is certainly applicable, but in context he is talking to Israel. I believe we can see that evident today. They are searching for the Messiah in the Torah, in the Talmud, but cannot grasp the simplicity of the gospel.

Something that I found interesting about this verse is that this day of the famine is future. We know that from the two statements, *"the days come,"* and *"I will send."* So there is something in the future that is coming from God that will prohibit them from hearing the word of God. Here is the interesting part. They are already not hearing, but this failure to hear that they are experiencing now is of their own choosing. This is similar to what John said happened in John chapter 12. The people refused to believe on God, so God hardened their hearts to the point that they could not believe.

What a dangerous position to get themselves into. They reject God over and over again until they get to the point that they cannot believe, they cannot repent. There is a famine of hearing, there is a turning over to the reprobate mind (Romans). Let this be a warning to each and every one of us!

No matter how or to what people you want to apply this verse to, the principle is apparent and applicable in every situation.

It can be seen with Saul, the first king of Israel. Saul disobeyed God's directions continually until Samuel finally informed Saul in I Samuel 15 that God had rejected him from being king.

Samuel passed away, and Saul was desperate to hear from God. He tried everything he knew to do so, but God would not answer him.

I Samuel 28:6

And when Saul enquired of the LORD, the LORD answered him not, neither by dreams, nor by Urim, nor by prophets.

We see this in the Jews at the end of the Old Testament. Even after going into Babylonian captivity, seeing God deliver them, restoring them to their land, and rebuilding the temple. Malachi tells us that they had again grown cold, callous, indifferent to God's words. So much so that they went into a 400 year drought, where they did not receive any word from God.

Fast forward to today. There is so much access to Bible and doctrine by means of books and the internet, but we have less power, less authority, and less fellowship with God. We are starving in the midst of spiritual abundance.

There was a case years ago of men that were living in the wilderness, and the area was abundant with rabbits so much that rabbit is the only thing that they ate. But after only a few months they mysteriously began to die of starvation even though they were eating as much rabbit as they wanted. It's called rabbit starvation, or protein toxicity. Our bodies cannot survive on just lean meat, there has to be a balance of fats involved with it.

By the same token, today we are up to our ears in commentaries, documentaries, and devotionals. We have a belly full of information, but most are starving spiritually because they will not digest it! They refuse to live according to the principles that God sets forth in His Word. They go into their spiritual studies with their own pre-conceived notion of who God is, and what God wants. They don't let God speak through His Word and direct their lives. So now we have all kinds of crazy doctrines and denominations out there because God has closed their understanding due to their disobedience.

This begs the question, why are they not finding God? Is God saying that he will hide himself from a people that are genuinely seeking after Him? I believe that the next verse answers this question for us.

Amos 8:12

And they shall wander from sea to sea, and from the north even to the east, they shall run to and fro to seek the word of the LORD, and shall not find it.

This is Israel, the NORTHERN tribes of Israel, that Amos is talking to. Notice the direction that they are searching. From sea to sea, Israel is flanked on either side by the Mediterranean Sea to the the west and the Sea of Galilee to the east. So they are looking for God in the bounds of their habitation, their rebellious and idolatrous habitation.

Then it says from the north and to the east. North of Israel and east of Israel are pagan lands. These are people that do not know the God of the Bible.

They are looking in every direction, except for where God is! The Word of the LORD was in the south! Judah was no saint, they had their own set of problems, but Judah and Jerusalem were south of Israel, that is where God was. That's where the true worship was to be carried out. That is where they left God when the kingdom split 150 plus years earlier. They weren't genuinely seeking after God, they knew EXACTLY where God was. They were looking for God in every other place and in every other thing except for where they knew Him to be!

This is why people cannot find God today. They search for Him in astronomy and science. They search for Him in everything except for where He is, in the pages of the King James Bible! Like Israel, they don't like God's rules, they don't like God's commandments. So they set out to create a *"kinder, gentler"* God. And because of this they are starving for truth.

Amos 8:13

In that day shall the fair virgins and young men faint for thirst.

Youth is associated with strength. John said the following in 1 John 2:14, *"I have written unto you, young men, because ye are strong, and the word of God abideth in you, and ye have overcome the wicked one."* But Amos is saying that even the young, the physically fit and active, will not be able to protect themselves in the day of judgment.

Isaiah mentions a similar situation to Judah.

Isaiah 40:30

Even the youths shall faint and be weary, and the young men shall utterly fall:

That's why Solomon told us to, *"trust in the Lord with all thine heart; and lean not unto thine own understanding. In all thy ways acknowledge Him, and He shall direct thy path."* Isaiah backs this up with this very next verse.

Isaiah 40:31

But they that wait upon the LORD shall renew their strength; they shall mount up with wings as eagles; they shall run, and not be weary; and they shall walk, and not faint.

Paul goes on to tell us in Ephesians;

Ephesians 6:10

Finally, my brethren, be strong in the Lord, and in the power of his might.

There are many more verses that we could cite about how we are to look to Christ and not ourselves. That's one of the many sins that Israel was guilty of that day, self reliance. Sadly, this is a sin that is killing most churches today as well.

Amos 8:14

14 They that swear by the sin of Samaria, and say, Thy god, O Dan, liveth; and, The manner of Beersheba liveth; even they shall fall, and never rise up again.

Notice the difference of what they are swearing by. Now this swearing is not what we would think of today but it simply means to *"promise upon an oath."* God has sworn three times in this book, or promised them on an oath. Twice he has sworn upon His name. In chapter 2 He "sworn by His holiness." In chapter 6 He *"sworn by himself."* But in chapter 8 He, *"sworn by the excellency of Jacob"* which is the pride of Israel. He is making a promise that is backed up with the authority of His name, and a promise of judgment on their sins.

Israel is promising upon an oath as well. But the authority of which they are swearing is significantly less than God's. They are swearing on the sin of Samaria. That would be like me promising you something based on the holy purity of Hollywood. Not too reassuring.

But notice the substance of their promise. They are so blinded by their idolatry that they are elevating the gold calf of Dan above the God of heaven. And the unscrupulous practices of Joel and Abiah, Samuels sons, and their perverting of judgment in Beersheba. They are exhaling them over the preaching of Amos.

Amos tells them that these will fall and never rise again. We know from history that this is exactly what happen.

PERSONAL NOTES

CHAPTER 9

Righteous Indignation

Amos 9:1

I saw the Lord standing upon the altar: and he said, Smite the lintel of the door, that the posts may shake: and cut them in the head, all of them; and I will slay the last of them with the sword: he that fleeth of them shall not flee away, and he that escapeth of them shall not be delivered.

We come to the final chapter of Amos, chapter 9. It would be great to say that Israel has heeded the warnings of Amos. It would be wonderful to read that they saw the error of their ways and repented like Ninevah did in the days of Jonah, but sadly this is not the case.

This people that came from the lineage of Abraham, that sold their younger brother into Egyptian slavery, and that went down to Egypt themselves and later became slaves to Egypt.

This people that God delivered by a mighty hand through the Red Sea, that saw Mount Sinai smolder and quake under the awesome power of an almighty God, who saw God provide for 40 years in the wilderness, and bring them into the promise land.

They are now in the position of the Egyptians, they are now the rejectors of God, and are about to face wrath from the same God that brought the plagues against Egypt. The reason I am using the example of Egypt is because that is the same language that God is using in verse 1. The application of the blood to the door posts that delivered them on the Passover, those door posts will now shake under the judgment of an almighty God.

Oh, it's not that Israel had always done right, but God had always had mercy. This is astounding considering their attitude toward God and their rebellion through the years. Moses even told them in his farewell address;

Deuteronomy 9:24

Ye have been rebellious against the LORD from the day that I knew you.

Through all of their complaining and rebellion against God, He still had mercy. The reason that God continually had mercy is because of their willingness to repent. But now they have gotten so hard hearted, so wicked, so depraved, and so wrapped up in themselves. They have refused the mercy of God so many times that they put God into a position that He can no longer stand by and let them get away with their sins. They have forced God's hand of judgment in their lives.

In the book of Revelation we see John constantly being taken around by an angel. In the book of Daniel God dispatches angels to deliver messages to Daniel about future events, and of coming deliverance. But here in Amos chapter 9, as in the beginning of chapter 8, we see that God Himself is measuring out the judgment against Israel.

Look at the place where that judgment is being delivered. It is at the altar. The altar was a place of sacrifice, where they were supposed to bring their offering to God to temporarily atone for their sins, in anticipation of the ultimate sacrifice to come.

But they had polluted the altar of God by building altars to false gods in Dan and Bethel. They had turned the use of the altar into theater instead of a heartfelt repentance to God. So God is now going to show them what He thinks of their unsanctioned altar and their idolatrous worship.

After the three year besiegement from Assyria where 90% of them die, and the remaining 10% are carried away into captivity. Just in case there were any that thought they might escape the besiegement. Just incase there are any that think they can hide and not be carried away into captivity. God tells them that he would personally see to it that they do not survive.

Amos 9:2

Though they dig into hell, thence shall mine hand take them; though they climb up to heaven, thence will I bring them down:

The "preppers" of today are getting ready for any kind of apocalyptic situation that may happen in our country. Be it war or natural disaster, they have their bug-out bags and bunkers stocked with beanie-weenies and Vienna sausages. But in this age of technology, satellites, surveillance, infrared capabilities, and facial recognition technology, can we really hide from the government anymore?

If it is that difficult to hide from man, how much harder is it to hide from the Creator of the universe? Yet many are still foolish enough to think that they can hide from God.

Amos 9:3

And though they hide themselves in the top of Carmel, I will search and take them out thence; and though they be hid from my sight in the bottom of the sea, thence will I command the serpent, and he shall bite them:

It is interesting that Amos mentions mount Carmel here. It rises up about 1800 miles into the sky. There are over 1000 caves in mount Carmel. A place that would be perfect for hiding from one's adversary. We saw a similar situation play out in the war in Afghanistan, when the Taliban armies were hiding out in the caves of the mountains. It was difficult for our soldiers to hunt down and find the enemy in all the caves that were in the mountains of that country. But what is difficult for man is easy for God. And even the height and caves of Carmel did not save Israel in that day.

Amos 9:4

And though they go into captivity before their enemies, thence will I command the sword, and it shall slay them: and I will set mine eyes upon them for evil, and not for good.

The guilty soul cannot escape the wrath of an almighty God. There is no depth that we can dive to or height that we can ascend to to escape the judgment of God.

Man thinks that through technology he can make himself immortal, but this King James Bible that has been proven true time and time again, it is also true in the statement that the writer of Hebrews makes.

Hebrews 9:27

And as it is appointed unto men once to die, but after this the judgment:

This passage in Amos also brings to light another solemn truth from the book of Hebrews.

Hebrews 10:31

It is a fearful thing to fall into the hands of the living God.

God is holy, just, and righteous, and He deserves our honor, respect, and adoration. However, Israel continually chose to go against the commandments of God not understanding that He will, *"set mine eyes upon them for evil, and not for good."*

This is similar language that God used in Deuteronomy.

Deuteronomy 11:26

Behold, I set before you this day a blessing and a curse;

27 A blessing, if ye obey the commandments of the LORD your God, which I command you this day:

28 And a curse, if ye will not obey the commandments of the LORD your God, but turn aside out of the way which I command you this day, to go after other gods, which ye have not known.

Oh, it's not that God was unjust or unfair to Israel. God gave them the choice. He spelled it out plainly through His servant Moses. Israel made their choice, He is now simply giving them what they wanted.

Amos 9:5

And the Lord GOD of hosts is he that toucheth the land, and it shall melt, and all that dwell therein shall mourn: and it shall rise up wholly like a flood; and shall be drowned, as by the flood of Egypt.

There are several things in this verse that have already been stated. But they are highlighted again for emphasis. First of all we see that it is God that is personally handing out the punishment.

Secondly, he emphasizes their mourning. Do not think that any punishment handed out by God will be a light thing. He is telling them, *"I don't think you really appreciate how bad this is going to be."* It is like He is making one final plea for them to get right with God.

Thirdly, he is again drawing comparisons to Egypt. Too many times we turn a blind eye to our own sin and only look at everyone else's. We get the attitude *"God is going to teach them a lesson,"* not realizing that we are in need of the same lesson. This is Israel's attitude here. They boasted and bragged to their children about God punishing Egypt not realizing that they were committing the same sins as Egypt did, and therefore were worthy of the same judgment.

There's one more thing to notice here before we move on to the next verse. There is a change in verse 5 from the first four verses of this final chapter. In these first 4 verses God is telling Israel what He is going to do. This is emphasized with the use of the words *"I will, or will I"* 6 different times.

As we get to verses 5 and 6, Amos confirms again, as he has several times in the book, the authority by which he speaks! Amos is making it clear that it is not his own authority, but God's! Verse 5 starts with, *"And the Lord God of hosts is He."* He gives His authority again four more times in the next verse with the words, *"it is He," "founded His troop," "He that calleth,"* and, *"The LORD is His name,"* further solidifying His authority as Judge.

Amos 9:6

It is he that buildeth his stories in the heaven, and hath founded his troop in the earth; he that calleth for the waters of the sea, and poureth them out upon the face of the earth: The LORD is his name.

So what is the illustration that God gives in verse 6 to demonstrate His authority? Well, He said that He buildeth His stories. When we talk about a multi level building we speak of "stories." In Genesis 6:16 the Bible talks about the stories in Noah's ark. We know that there are three stories (levels) to the heavens, and knowing that the dimensions of the New Jerusalem are 1500 miles cubed. I'm sure there are some "stories" there as well. But regardless, I believe His point is simply this, He is the Creator of it all, from top to bottom. He is the Creator.

Then He said that He *"hath founded His troop in the earth."* From the heavens to the earth, He is stating His supreme authority over all creation. He controls the evaporation cycles and the storms that rain down upon the earth, *"he that calleth for the waters of the sea, and poureth them out upon the face of the earth."* He ends the verse with His personal affirmation, *"The LORD is His name."*

Amos 9:7

Are ye not as children of the Ethiopians unto me, O children of Israel? saith the LORD. Have not I brought up Israel out of the land of Egypt? and the Philistines from Caphtor, and the Syrians from Kir?

God really gives them a gut punch here. Jews can naturally be very arrogant. Someone once said that if you have 2 Jews you have 3 views. They are very opinionated and convinced that their way is right. It's clear from reading the Scriptures that this is a character trait that they have carried down through the centuries. And they especially considered themselves better than the Ethiopians, those ole dirty descendants of Ham. One only has to look at how they treated Moses wife to see that this is true.

Numbers 12:1

And Miriam and Aaron spake against Moses because of the Ethiopian woman whom he had married: for he had married an Ethiopian woman.

Have you ever accused someone of something or complained about someone to another person, only to have that person throw it right back in your face and point out that you are doing something that is just as bad or worse?

The Jews did not like the Ethiopians and had no problem letting everyone know about it, but God said to Israel, *"you're just like them in my sight."* Ouch! What a reality check!

Amos 9:8

Behold, the eyes of the Lord GOD are upon the sinful kingdom, and I will destroy it from off the face of the earth; saving that I will not utterly destroy the house of Jacob, saith the LORD.

He calls Israel a sinful kingdom in verse 8. What a contrast from what God wanted them to be!

Exodus 19:5

Now therefore, if ye will obey my voice indeed, and keep my covenant, then ye shall be a peculiar treasure unto me above all people: for all the earth is mine:

6 And ye shall be unto me a kingdom of priests, and an holy nation. These are the words which thou shalt speak unto the children of Israel.

But they didn't obey His voice, so judgment is coming. That brings to mind David's solemn lamentation over king Saul, *"How are the mighty fallen."*

The next phrase only gets darker, as he goes on to say, *"I will destroy it from off the face of the earth."* If this is where the story were to stop, if the book of Amos ended right here, the replacement theologians of our day would have some what of a leg to stand on. (They actually wouldn't, there are plenty other passages in the Bible that refute this position, but that statement sounded dramatic). Because it has all been doom and gloom until this point of the chapter.

God tells them that they have nowhere to hide, that He WILL bring judgment upon them. Although they've been worshiping false gods, He confirms that He is the true and living God, *"the LORD is His name."* That they are to Him what they consider the Ethiopians to be to them.

All this heaviness and negativity that has been in this chapter and even throughout the majority of this book, culminates with the statement that He will *"destroy it (Israel) from off the face of the earth."* But this is not where this verse, chapter, or book ends!

The next statement He says, *"saving that I will not utterly destroy the house of Jacob."* So, although they are about to go into captivity, God is saying that there is still yet a future plan for Israel. Fortunately Amos does not leave us hanging in suspended animation because the last 7 verses of this book are some of the most interesting, hopeful, and exciting verses of the book of Amos.

A National Sifting

Amos 9:9

For, lo, I will command, and I will sift the house of Israel among all nations, like as corn is sifted in a sieve, yet shall not the least grain fall upon the earth.

This is an amazing verse! When Israel went into captivity they did not go into all the nations of the earth, they went into

Assyria. Later Assyria fell to Babylon, but Israel did not return to their land. That's not to say that there were not some stragglers that eventually returned, but they did not come back to reclaim the land that God had promised to their respective tribes. We can only speculate as to where they went during this time, but we must keep our speculation Bible based. So, when the Bible says that they would be sifted among all nations, sifted means to be moved about, we can rest assured that this is exactly what happened.

Their cousin Judah later joined them in that sifting after the Jews rejected the Messiah and Jerusalem was destroyed in 70AD. Many people go to the Holocaust as the prime example of God's "sifting" of the Jews, and it is a strong example. However, it is not the only example of Israel being sifted or "moved" throughout the nations of the world.

In 70AD. Jerusalem was destroyed, and the Jews were scattered.

In 135AD. The Roman emperor Hadrian came to power and thus controlled the land of Israel. He proclaimed an edict that Jews were not to be allowed back to the city, and any that tried it were to be executed.

In 1096AD. Jews were branded as enemies of Christianity. 12,000 were killed along Rhine river in Germany. (Hitler was not the first German to kill the Jews).

In 1181AD. King Phillip of France banished the Jews from their country, robbing them of their homes, possession's, and property.

In 1189AD. After the coronation of Richard the Lionhearted, many Jews were murdered and their possession's seized for the crown. (Long live the king).

In 1348AD. Jews were blamed for the Black Plague in England, and many were killed.

In 1478AD. the Spanish Inquisition began. A few years later in 1492, the same time that "Chris" Columbus sailed the ocean blue, 300,000 Jews were banished from Spain.

In 1520AD. Jews were banished from Naples, Venice, and other cities in Italy.

In 1794AD. Jewish men in Russia were forced to serve 25 years in the Russian military.

In 1903AD. Again in Russia, the Pogroms took place, and many Jews were massacred and their villages destroyed.

Then finally in the 1930's and 1940's we have the Holocaust.

Notice the nations that were mentioned here, the Roman Empire, Germany, France, England, Spain, Italy, Russia. Maybe the Bible is true when God said through Amos that they would be *"sifted among the nations!"*

Now the replacement theologian will say that when they were scattered through the nations that they lost their identity, their lineage was mired, and there's no way that we can tell who the real Israelites are. But the last part of verse 9 teaches the very opposite of that! *"yet shall not the least grain fall upon the earth."* God is saying that through this sifting that the seed of Israel will be preserved not lost!

Amos 9:10

All the sinners of my people shall die by the sword, which say, The evil shall not overtake nor prevent us.

The previous verse (9) tells us that Israel will be preserved through the sifting. It's ok if you don't understand what happen to the tribes of Judah, Issachar, Levi, and the other 9 tribes. You and I don't have to understand, we don't have to know. God knows, all we have to do is to trust Him!

But now verse 10 tells us that the sinners will not escape either. Not just the heathen sinners, but sinners of *"my people,"* the Israelites. There is a group today that teaches that we should not waste our time trying to evangelize Jews, that they will all be saved. The only problem with that theory is that it is unbiblical.

Jew or Gentile, black or white, male or female, young or old, rich or poor, there is no respecter of persons with God. Man may deal unfairly, we see that even in our country today. Politicians get away with crimes that you and I would be thrown under the jail for because of who they are, or who their financial backers are. That will not happen with God. He is a just and fair judge. Sin is dealt with regardless of political, ethnic, or financial status.

A Glorious Regathering

Amos 9:11

In that day will I raise up the tabernacle of David that is fallen, and close up the breaches thereof; and I will raise up his ruins, and I will build it as in the days of old:

Amos starts this verse out with the phrase, *"in that day."* He also uses that phrase several times in this book, including the preceding chapter. In chapter 8 *"in that day"* was something dark and gloomy, but here it is something to look forward to, further emphasizing my point that the day of the Lord is not a 24 hour day, but a period of time.

Amos is speaking of the day of the Lord here. It is mentioned for the first time in the bible in Isaiah 2:12 (Isaiah was a contemporary of Amos). But the first time chronologically that it is mentioned is in Joel. Joel lived 60-70 years before Amos. So if Joel was the first to use this term, then we know that this terminology of *"the day of the Lord"* is a fairly new concept to Israel during Amos' day. And this is what Joel said about it.

Joel 1:15

Alas for the day! for the day of the LORD is at hand, and as a destruction from the Almighty shall it come.

Isaiah says;

Isaiah 2:12

For the day of the LORD of hosts shall be upon every one that is proud and lofty, and upon every one that is lifted up; and he shall be brought low:

In the verses following verse 12 he goes on to state that it (the day of the Lord) will be upon the high cedars, upon the oaks of Bashan, and upon the high mountains. He said that the loftiness of man will be brought low, and the Lord shall be exalted.

Keep in mind when Israel reads this passage they could only see judgment happening to their enemies, and not to them. They thought they were safe because they were God's chosen. So a few years later when Amos comes along in chapter 5, Amos has to tell them that the day of the Lord is not good for them.

Amos 5:18

Woe unto you that desire the day of the LORD! to what end is it for you?

And again in verse 20.

Amos 5:20

Shall not the day of the LORD be darkness, and not light? even very dark, and no brightness in it?

By the time that Amos got to town they were looking forward to the day of the Lord, while still living in their sins. Amos has to tell them that this day of the Lord is not going to be good for them if they do not correct their evil ways.

I believe that the day of the Lord starts after the rapture of the church, goes on through the tribulation period, and all the way through the millennial. So the beginning of "that day" will not be good for them, but it turns out good in the end!

So he said, *"In that day will I raise up the tabernacle of David that is fallen."* He is saying that even though Israel will be sifted, God will restore them again.

James, during their big debate in Acts 15 in Jerusalem, quotes from the last chapter of Amos.

Acts 15:14
Simeon hath declared how God at the first did visit the Gentiles, to take out of them a people for his name.
15 And to this agree the words of the prophets; as it is written,
16 After this I will return, and will build again the tabernacle of David, which is fallen down; and I will build again the ruins thereof, and I will set it up:
17 That the residue of men might seek after the Lord, and all the Gentiles, upon whom my name is called, saith the Lord, who doeth all these things.

What is most interesting about what James said in Acts 15 is not his quotation of Amos, but what he said in the verses leading up to the quotation of Amos. James said that Simon (Peter) declared God had visited the Gentiles, and he's going to take a people out of them for His name. James was careful to show that the prophets agree with this statement. These are his statements in verses 14 and 15. He starts the quotation of Amos in verse 16, but James starts the verse out a little differently than Amos does. Amos says, *"In that day will I raise up the tabernacle of David."* James says, *"After this I will return and will build again the tabernacle of David."* So the question is, who is correct? They both are! James is giving clarification to what Amos is speaking about. The key word in James statement is the word, *"after."* He is saying that after Christ has assembled His Gentile bride, that God will again turn and deal with the Jewish people. Amos further emphasizes the *"after effect"* in verse 12.

Amos 9:12

That they may possess the remnant of Edom, and of all the heathen, which are called by my name, saith the LORD that doeth this.

Keep in mind that he is speaking to Israel, not Judah in this particular passage. 120 years after Israel goes into Assyrian captivity, Judah goes into Babylonian captivity. Judah came out of captivity, but Israel never has. Since Israel has going into Assyrian captivity in 722bc, we have never seen them gathered back into the land to fulfill these verses of Amos until May 14th, 1948, when Israel became a nation again.

Amos 9:13

Behold, the days come, saith the LORD, that the plowman shall overtake the reaper, and the treader of grapes him that soweth seed; and the mountains shall drop sweet wine, and all the hills shall melt.

Verse 11 tells us that God will raise up the tabernacle of David. Verse 12 tells us that they will possess the land again. Verse 13 tells us that once they do possess this land that it will produce, and produce bountifully! Isaiah is in agreement with Amos.

Isaiah 35:1

The wilderness and the solitary place shall be glad for them; and the desert shall rejoice, and blossom as the rose.

Isaiah 27:6

He shall cause them that come of Jacob to take root: Israel shall blossom and bud, and fill the face of the world with fruit.

What makes this even more exciting, what just puts the cherry on top, is that history confirms this too! Now, we don't need physical evidence, we ought to take the Bible by faith. But how wonderful when we can look and see historical evidence of these things coming to pass!

Before 1948, the Ottoman Empire (Turkey) had possession of the Land of Israel. During that time, they could not grow so much as a weed. They could produce no fruits or vegetables of any kind. The average rain fall in the land for hundreds of years was less than 11 inches annually. That is considered to be extreme drought territory. Isaiah tells us that it would be that way!

Isaiah 5:6

And I will lay it waste: it shall not be pruned, nor digged; but there shall come up briers and thorns: <u>I will also command the clouds that they rain no rain upon it.</u>

But now, since 1948, the average annual rainfall is over double that, and Israel is a world leader in the production of fruits and vegetables! In 2025 the fruit and vegetable market of Israel is 6.26 billion dollars, and expected to be at 7.72 billion by 2030! Bible prophecy is being fulfilled right in front of our eyes! Most Christians are just too concerned with sports and entertainment to even notice!

Amos goes on to further expound on this in the following verse.

Amos 9:14

And I will bring again the captivity of my people of Israel, and they shall build the waste cities, and inhabit them; and they shall plant vineyards, and drink the wine thereof; they shall also make gardens, and eat the fruit of them.

It amazes me how people can read these verses, and not see God's future plan for Israel. Just as in the previous verses, we have witnessed the verse being fulfilled in just the past 80 years. This verse was never fulfilled until 1948.

Amos 9:15

And I will plant them upon their land, and they shall no more be pulled up out of their land which I have given them, saith the LORD thy God.

It took almost 2700 years, but God fulfilled His promise of verse 14, to restore Israel back to their land. And the same God that is powerful enough to restore them back to the land as He promised them in verse 14 is powerful enough to keep the promise that He made to them in verse 15. They will no more be pulled out of the land.

As of the writing of this book, fall of 2025, Israel is a wicked Godless nation. They are assembled as God's national people, but they are currently enemies of the Gospel as Paul stated in Romans 11:28. They are currently like the dry bones of Ezekiel chapter 37, they are standing as a great army, but there is no breath in them. But one of these days during the tribulation, that time of Jacobs trouble. God will once again deal with the Jewish people.

PERSONAL NOTES

PERSONAL NOTES

Made in the USA
Coppell, TX
09 March 2026

73430012R00121